A PHILOSOPHY OF SIMPLE LIVING

A
PHILOSOPHY
OF SIMPLE LIVING

Jérôme Brillaud

REAKTION BOOKS

For Ethan

Published by Reaktion Books Ltd
Unit 32, Waterside
44–48 Wharf Road
London N1 7UX, UK

www.reaktionbooks.co.uk

First published 2020
Copyright © Jérôme Brillaud 2020

Printed and bound in Great Britain
by TJ International, Padstow, Cornwall

A catalogue record for this book is available from the British Library

ISBN 978 1 78914 227 3

CONTENTS

INTRODUCTION:
WHAT'S IN A NAME?

A simple mode of life is nowadays difficult, requiring as it does
far more reflection and gift for invention than even very clever
people possess. The most honourable will perhaps still say, 'I
have not the time for such lengthy reflection. The simple life
is for me too lofty a goal: I will wait till those wiser than I have
discovered it.'

FRIEDRICH NIETZSCHE, *The Wanderer and His Shadow*[1]

For many people, confusion and uncertainty create a desire for
simplicity that leads to a futile longing to return to basic values
and foundational beliefs. In today's world, however, simplicity
has become an idle dream that no longer can be realized.

MARK C. TAYLOR, *The Moment of Complexity*[2]

This book is for those who still believe that a simple life is
neither just a lofty goal for the wise nor the object of the
futile longing of dreamers. That said, there might be some truth
to Nietzsche's statement, but only if the goals of the simple life
are set so high that simplicity must remain an ideal, and only if
we are willing to hand over the task of thinking about simple

living to those who are wiser, whoever they may be. But ours is neither a time for unattainable goals nor a time for the passive reception of ideas. There is enough evidence to show that blind quixotism cannot end well; passivity does not bode well either. Ours is a time for action. This book was born out of the conviction that a simple – or simpler – life is not just possible but desirable, because among other things it is a life one chooses.

Another intention motivated the pages that follow. For millennia, men and women have devoted their lives to simplicity. Some of them retreated from the world in order to live simply; others attained a degree of active simplicity verging on martyrdom; still others wrote books or founded philosophies on simplicity – while a great many lived simple lives requiring little explicit commitment or bookish wisdom. Their lives, their accounts of simple living, their ideas and theories, have inspired these pages. These lives, some of which were truly exceptional, testify to the great variety of experiences and ideas to be found under the rubric of simple living. Some common themes emerge from the theories and practices of simplicity; however, it was not my intent to develop a general theory or write a grand narrative of simple living. To study 'the neutral', Roland Barthes chose to collate the meanings of the term – to name it rather than to define it.[3] My intention was similar. A normative definition of simple living which would set forth rules culminating in a to-do list would be reductive. My interest lay in the various manifestations of simple living at different moments in history, in different types of lived experiences and in discourses that fit under the name 'simple living'. 'It would seem we can approach simplicity only indirectly, by something other than itself,' wrote André Comte-Sponville in *A Small Treatise on the Great Virtues*.[4] My book may offer just that – an indirect approach to simplicity as it is manifested in simple living.

The term 'simple living' conjures up the ideas of living, life and simplicity. Taken together, and prima facie, these three ideas seem to interlock readily, forming a sensible causal chain: living simply leads to the simple life. Yet, the three ideas do not coexist in perfect harmony in the compounded term. In fact, the disparity between life and simplicity has never been more marked than it is today. And, as we know, 'living' means more than just being alive. The distinction between 'living' and 'life' has a long and complicated history. In their investigations into the nature of life, Greek philosophers from Thales to Aristotle attempted to identify the general principles animating all living beings. They arrived at different conclusions. In the sixth century BCE, Thales, for one, found that water was the *archē* or single origin and unchanging principle of all things; for Anaximenes it was air. For Descartes in the seventeenth century, life sprang from the interaction between physical mechanisms and the mind. Against a purely mechanistic view of life, early modern vitalists maintained that life was energized by a non-physical principle. Today, life is generally understood as a complex system that self-maintains, self-constructs and self-reproduces. Life systems subject to natural selection respond to the complex environments in which they emerge. Molecular biology is now providing answers that to all appearances render obsolete the old philosophical question 'what is life?' The idea that the complexity of life is irreducible to one principle dominates the scientific community. On the other hand, this notion seems to cause many laypeople to surrender the effort to understand it: 'life is so complex – better leave it to the scientists.' The scientific consensus, the categorization and appropriation of knowledge, and the dismissal of questions related to life dangerously undermine the idea, perhaps the possibility itself, of a simple life. If life is biologically complex, can it be lived simply? Is a simple life the stuff of dreamt-up theories from the past? Are life and simplicity irreconcilable?

For centuries, natural scientists have debated whether life was governed by simple rules. 'The story of science is that of repeated revolutions in our conception of the simple,' wrote Jack Cohen and Ian Stewart in their book *The Collapse of Chaos: Discovering Simplicity in a Complex World*.[5] Until recent times, the simplicity of a scientific theory was the criterion for its acceptance or rejection. Reductionism has long been and will continue to be a bone of contention for scientists and historians of science. Isaac Newton famously said that 'nature is pleased with simplicity, and affects not the pomp of superfluous causes.'[6] Already in the eighteenth century, however, scientists questioned the validity of simplicity as an epistemological virtue. Georg Christoph Lichtenberg, a German physicist known for his discovery of the rudimentary principles of xerographic copying – and for his aphorisms – defiantly wrote: 'The lofty simplicity of nature all too often rests on the plain simplicity of the one who thinks he sees it.'[7] Newton's universe and Descartes' method, both founded on the principle of simplicity, were considered by certain natural philosophers of the eighteenth century to be established on mere bias.

One of the most compelling and thorough challenges to Cartesian simplicity was penned by the French philosopher Gaston Bachelard in the early twentieth century. For Descartes, a proposition or phenomenon has to be self-evident in order to be simple. Bachelard proposed that there are no simple phenomena, but rather that every phenomenon consists of a fabric of relations.

Consequently, there is no such thing as a simple nature or a simple substance: a substance is rather a network of attributes. He adds that there are no simple ideas, because no idea can be understood until it has been integrated into a complex system of thoughts and experiences. For Bachelard, there is no simplicity per se; there are only simplifications. While simple ideas may have some heuristic or pedagogical value, such ideas cannot serve as the basis for scientific knowledge or truth. In Bachelard's words, 'simple ideas are in fact simplifications of more complex truths.'[8] In 1928 he asserted that simplicity is never a state of things, natural or otherwise, but a state of mind, thus echoing the eighteenth-century German physicist Georg Christoph Lichtenberg. One does not believe something is simple because it is simple; it is simple because one believes it is so.[9] For Bachelard and many others after him, simplicity is an erroneous belief system unreservedly endorsed by unscientific minds. He did not put an end to the debate. Lawrence B. Slobodkin, one of the forerunners of modern ecology, stated that 'no organism responds to the full complexity of its environment.'[10] We simplify when we listen, feel and watch.[11] Whether it is a constitutive element of biological life or a figment of our fertile imaginations – scientific or not – simplicity affects us in ways that are beyond the scope of this study. It is enough to pause at the provisional conclusions that life is complex and that our perceptions of it might result from simplifications which significantly compromise any holistic understanding of life itself.

While the natural sciences are concerned with biological life, philosophy has traditionally turned her attention to 'the good life'. The good life constitutes the *telos* of ethics, which regulate individual conduct. It is also the ideal towards which politics supposedly strive. Early in the *Politics*, Aristotle considers the correlation between biological life, described as 'the bare needs of life', and 'the good life': 'When several villages are united in a single complete community, large enough or quite self-sufficing, the state comes into existence, originating in the bare needs of life, and continuing in existence for the sake of the good life.'[12] In this example and later in the *Politics*, the good life (*bios*) is shown to emerge from 'the bare needs of life' (*zoē*).[13] Although political life is derived from this 'bare life', the ancient Greeks largely banned the latter from politics, confining it to the *oikos*, the household. Giorgio Agamben sees in this exclusion one of the differences between ancient and modern ideas of democracy:

> If anything characterizes modern democracy as opposed to classical democracy, then, it is that modern democracy presents itself from the beginning as a vindication and liberation of *zoē*, and that it is constantly trying to transform its own bare life into a way of life and to find, so to speak, the *bios* of *zoē*.[14]

The conversion of the 'bare life' into an organized way of life for both the individual and the community is not a smooth process of assimilation with a clear end result. In some cases, it has led, paradoxically, to the complete subjugation and annihilation of biological life for the sake of a 'better way of life'. Ecological disasters resulting from political decisions provide many examples of the destruction of human and non-human lives. DNA registration of children displaying behaviours that have the potential to evolve into criminal activities is an example of the politicization of biological life studied by Agamben. In such cases, life is exposed to the perpetuation of potential violence by biopolitical powers.

The politics of life – or 'biopolitics' – creating, regulating and destroying life in the name of life itself, is an aporia for modern democracies. The apparent conflict between the two aspects of 'life' – life as a complex, ever-changing system and the good life as a complex political system aspiring to stability – is not disappearing anytime soon. In reality, political systems have justified their existence and their operations by an appeal to the alleged naturalness of needs they actually generate and promote. If private property were to be found in nature, then surely capitalism would be natural. The real tension between a manufactured ideal presented as necessary for the life of the community and a life that resists empirical description and scientific investigation remains unresolved.

There is another division between the two conceptions of life which pertains to our discussion of simplicity. The metabolic life that runs through our veins without our paying much attention to it – except when it is disrupted or coming to an end – is outshone by the idea of the life that transcends the organic and extends into the great beyond. It bears different names – 'the life of the soul' is one example; it is the eternally disembodied life which looks down on the lower and perishable physical life. This higher form of life which transcends the pulsating life has long served as a beacon for those seeking to live in simplicity regardless of their religious inclinations. For instance, in the simplicity of their lives, monks strive to emulate the simple life of their God. For the monastic, mortal life is experienced as a preparatory spiritual exercise leading to eternal life.

In his *Philosophy of Living*, François Jullien makes the distinction between life which is determined from the outside and living. External determinations like birth, death, biological, ethical, political and eternal life help us conceptualize life.[15] Life can be organized into distinct categories, each with its own object and knowledge. Living, according to Jullien, escapes determination and categorization:

> 'Living' does not allow dissociation into various levels, nor does it authorize exteriority; upon it no backwards step is possible. Have we not been committed to this 'living', isolated and without landmarks, ever since what is always, for each of us, the dawn of time, and without our being able simply to imagine that it could ever be otherwise? We are unable to conceive of not living. Because 'to live', in the infinitive, is that anonymous nominal which right away withdraws all support of difference, whether of subjects or conjugation, from thought, and only retains its activity; but in so continual and discreet a way that we do not experience it as activity. Living is that eternal silence, implied right within us without our understanding it.[16]

Living acts quietly in us, so quietly that it is easy to stop hearing it, and heeding it. Those who have chosen to live simply remain attuned to the quiet activity of living that transpires in and around them. In many of the cases studied here, simple living consists in quieting the noise of a busy life in order to hear the soft sounds that are emitted by life. Once heard, the quiet activity that animates all living beings erases differences to create a world which is experienced as onefold – etymologically, as a simple world. The word 'simplicity' comes from the Latin *simplex* via the French *simplicité*. It originates in the Proto-Indo-European *sem* ('one') + *plek* ('to plait'), referring to that which is onefold or whole.[17]

When it is heard, the soft sound of living in us and around us unifies all that is separated by conceptual categories.

'Living' is the name for the quiet energy vitalized and experienced in the practice of simplicity as a way of life. Paying attention to all the varied forms of life, not just those that are sanctified, constitutes one of the first steps towards simple living. Attention to all living forms reveals a world inhabited by beings that have not been placed on this earth solely for the sake of human whim and profit. Those who, like the Quaker John Woolman, pay attention to life in its smallest manifestations, understand that care thrives in reciprocity and mutualism. Then one's attention turns to the care for all that lives. As a therapeutic principle, simplicity heals by making whole again that which was fractured – the words 'healing' and 'whole' share a common etymology. The term 'simples', which is rarely used today, evokes the curative properties of simplicity. 'Simples' refers to a range of medicinal plants used for their therapeutic properties since time immemorial: medieval monastic gardens, for example, had a section dedicated to them. Simples were remedies derived from a single unaltered source, mostly vegetal, but they could also be of animal or mineral origin. They differed from *composita* or electuaries, remedies in which, for instance, a single medicinal element is mixed with honey to make a palatable concoction. Simple remedies prescribed by herbalists were governed by the principle of similitudes, *similia similibus curantur*, 'like is cured by like'. In the sixteenth century, the Swiss alchemist Paracelsus developed the doctrine of 'signatures' or *signa naturae*, which stipulates that the physical appearance of a plant, or its habitat, dictates its medicinal virtue: the similarity of the shape or colour of the plant to the features of the disease or wound to be treated determined the selection of the simple to be used. In the spirit of healing mutualism promulgated by the medicinal theories of simples, all living beings help each other. Life heals life holistically. Wholeness, similarity and simplicity are related, in etymology as well as in herbalism, to health, vigour and vital energy – energy that is renewed and preserved by simples.[18]

Simple living has also been associated with the systematic disruption of perceived social unity and progress. Social conventions, which form the bases of life understood as a set of precepts and habits, have indeed been put to the test by the adepts of a simple life. The Cynics of the fourth century BCE provide one of the earliest and most famous examples of simple living with their tireless questioning of established values and customs. Throughout history, the name Diogenes has been attributed pejoratively to advocates of simple living, as if to underline their alleged maladaptation to life in society. Because the so-called later Cynics were suspicious of conventions readily embraced by the many, they were themselves suspected of antisocial behaviours and indoctrination. Often they were accused of preferring the ideal to a reality when in fact they were seeking reality behind the falsity of convention. They did not place their trust in unattainable ideals. Nor did they trust the world of arbitrary convention and rapid mechanization, which stifles life. In living simply, they found humility in the palpable organicity and wholesomeness of life.

In most cases simple living starts with a decision to reform one's life. Embracing the sanctity of life in all beings and questioning the arbitrariness of convention motivates some people to change the course of their lives. Their life reforms lead to the conclusion that living simply is not simply living. Instead, simple living arises with the decision to live deliberately rather than passively. In that sense, simple living remains inherently political. When it is enacted in every decision made, the awareness of living is no longer muted by busyness and habits. As a nascent movement, simple living can be described as the will to hear the murmur of life, served by the readiness to act. The degree of activism of those who have elected a simple life varies greatly. Some have retreated from the world of consumerism; others have just reduced their impulse to buy. This is a start. However, politicizing the decision to live simply may well be a matter of urgency. As a movement, Voluntary Simplicity is gaining ground, but it is also derailed by a multitude of expedients masquerading as simple living. Certain false prophets of simplicity are perhaps emblematic of our times, but their words and actions meet with the resistance of an increasing number of dedicated 'simplifiers'. Chapter Five testifies to that new trend.

This book shows some of the many forms of simplicity as a way of life. Ideas organizing simple lives have sometimes coalesced into ideologies, some of which have had dire consequences and have caused much harm. But the vast majority of people who endorse simple living also support social justice and the ethics of care, self-care and care for all living beings. Sometimes their suspicion of non-living things translates into a concern about unchecked technology. Restraint from excess in all its manifestations constitutes one of the perennial values of simple living. Another of these values is ingenuity, understood as the ability to see beyond the exclusive purpose conventionally assigned to objects. Repurposing has been present in simple living since its earliest appearance. Diogenes lived in a *pithos*, or jar, after all. Similarly, the spirit of inventiveness animates the lives of the American Shakers. Creating or repurposing in order to simplify one's life is also discussed in this book.

On 29 March 1827 Goethe wrote to the composer Carl Friedrich Zelter, his long-time friend:

> On a recent occasion, which I may perhaps ere long specify more particularly, I said, '*Il faut croire à la simplicité*', which means, one must believe in simplicity, in what is simple, in what is originally productive, if one wants to go the right way. This however is not granted to everyone; we are born in an artificial state, and it is far easier to make it more artificial still, than to return to what is simple.[19]

Aesthetic simplicity, whether it is defined as an original creative energy gracing the few as in this letter, is not addressed in these pages. Minimalism in the arts was beyond the scope of a study on simple living. Minimalism may contribute to a simple life and to an extent support it; it may also tap into some of the ideas expressed here, but it does not contribute directly to some of the more pressing philosophical issues this book hopes to address.

A more obvious omission from this account of simple living was a treatment of lived simplicity emerging from and enriching the various Eastern philosophical traditions. *A Philosophy of Simple Living* centres on episodes of the long history of simplicity as a way of life in Europe, America and the parts of the world they colonized. Some readers may also wonder why simplicity as a theoretical virtue receives little attention. The focus, however, is on lived experiences of simplicity and some of the ideas that sustain them rather than on the validity or elegance of arguments and theories. I have likewise refrained from casting a moral judgement on the accounts and theories of simple living reported in the pages that follow.

There are a few other things that this book does not claim to be. It is not a nostalgic song for long-lost days when people allegedly led simpler lives. If some of the accounts of simple lives reported here may inspire readers to live more simply, all the better. But proselytism was not the intention behind these pages. And this is not intended to be yet another self-help book on how to declutter one's life. Finally, this is not a book on the history of sustainable living. For much of human history, simple living was divorced from immediate environmental concerns, because up until the late eighteenth century, the world was not the object of insatiable greed on such a rapacious scale as it is today. Among other things, the term 'simple living' encompasses ideas of self-sufficiency and autonomy, deliberation and liberation, contiguity and wholeness, attention and care, as well as naming things for what they are. 'Saving the planet' is increasingly heard as the rallying cry of those engaged in simple living, and rightly so. But a life lived in simplicity also prizes freedom, justice, humility, critical thinking and care for others, human or not. Simple living is many things because it is experienced differently.

The oldest oracle in ancient Greece was communicated through the rustling of the leaves of a sacred oak dedicated to Gaia, the earth. Starting with the ancient world at Dodona, this book proceeds to the simple lives of the monks of early Christianity, whose intention is echoed in the anti-technology Christian writings of the past century. The third chapter focuses on the lived simplicity of the Shakers and Quakers in the seventeenth and eighteenth centuries in England and America and their legacy of simplicity. With the advent of the Industrial Revolution, the plea for simpler lives was made by Rousseau and Thoreau; their ideas and experiments make up Chapter Four. The final chapter looks at the much-needed contributions of voluntary simplifiers to better society and secure the future of the planet. Today more than ever, simplicity has been wholesaled to customers in dire need of simpler lives. For a great profit, simplicity is made easy for us.

As a term, 'simple living' is not affected by the unattainable and divisive ideals evoked by the substantive 'life', nor does it display a preoccupation with the inscrutable biological complexity of life. As an idea, simple living does not pretend to provide a solution to the tensions between biological life and the good life, whether political, ethical or religious. It does not conspire to expunge one life in the name of another. Simple living refers to lives in which the biological complements the political, where life and 'the good life' work in tandem to create new lives and to preserve existing ones. As a practice, it starts with listening to the soft sound of life in all that lives.

ONE

SIMPLE BEGINNINGS

The story has it that Theuth, the Egyptian god of invention, brought a gift to king Thamus. 'O King,' said Theuth, 'here is something that, once learned, will make the Egyptians wiser and will improve their memory; I have discovered a potion for memory and for wisdom.'[1] This magical potion is the written word. The king, however, did not share the god's enthusiasm. Theuth, who had concocted the elixir, could not cast an objective eye on his own invention, thought the king, nor could he decide without bias the merits of the gift of writing; only an 'external judge' could assess the gift and deliberate on its properties and virtues. Thamus feared that, contrary to the god's promise, the written word might increase forgetfulness instead of improving memory. For readers, he thought, might come to rely on sentences and knowledge they had not produced themselves, but had only read. 'You provide your students with the appearance of wisdom, not with its reality,' objected Thamus. 'They will imagine that they have come to know much while for the most part they will know nothing.'[2] Thamus tells the difference between knowledge that comes from within – remembered knowledge – and knowledge that relies on external signs – recollected knowledge. True knowledge, he concludes, is neither imparted by someone nor acquired from someone, but originates in us. The dialogue between the god and the king on the nature, foundation and dissemination of knowledge started with a gift we now take for granted, a potion to which our most celebrated values, such as the freedom of the printed word, are indebted. But the stories of inventions such as writing, with their touted promises of a better life, have always raised the spectre of endless complications, the extinction of old ways and irreversible modifications of abilities, whether physical or mental. The story of Theuth and Thamus is no exception.

This story of the divine gift of writing, narrated by Socrates, appears in Plato's *Phaedrus*. Before Socrates and his young interlocutor Phaedrus discuss the benefits and perils of the written word, the student asks his teacher whether the story of Theuth and Thamus is true or whether he created it for the sole purpose of his argument:

> But, my friend, replies Socrates, the priests of the temple of Zeus at Dodona say that the first prophecies were the words of an oak. Everyone who lived at the time, not being as wise as you young ones are today, found it rewarding enough in their simplicity to listen to an oak or even a stone, so long as it was telling the truth, while it seems to make a difference to you, Phaedrus, who is speaking and where he comes from. Why, though, don't you just consider whether what he says is right or wrong?[3]

Traditionally, the oracles at Dodona were simpler than those uttered at Delphi, which dealt with affairs of state. Dodona oracles were expressed in an unequivocal 'yes' or 'no'. They concerned simpler matters related to domestic and personal lives. The priests of Dione and Zeus at Dodona were said to sleep on the ground. They would not wash the dirt off their feet so as to remain in direct and permanent contact with the earth.[4] Philostratus the Elder (*fl.* third century CE) describes them as 'living from hand to mouth'; their 'picked-up livelihood', he reports, pleased their tutelar deities.[5] The priests' simple ways allowed the esoteric messages of their gods to be received without the interference of material concerns and written knowledge. Nothing in their simple lives obstructed the channels of communication with Zeus and the goddess Dione, whose messages sounded in the rustling of leaves or in the wind chimes hanging in the trees. For the priests, life enabled knowledge, an idea generally foreign to us today. For us, knowledge enables life. What one knows dictates how one lives. For them, living a simple life made knowing truths and ciphering messages possible.

Trees and stones revealed the truth to those who lived in simplicity. The Greek word for simplicity in this excerpt from *Phaedrus* is εὐήθεια, an ambivalent term that means whole-heartedness and guilelessness, as well as silliness. In the context of Socrates' argument, the word can be understood as a natural disposition to guilelessness or artlessness. The simple person who cares not about how messages are conveyed or whence they come will be better disposed to see the revealed truth wherever, when-ever and however it manifests itself. People living in simplicity like the priests accept the truth as it is, unadorned and simple in form and content. Artful minds who care more about how the truth appears than what it conveys will be blind to it. The achieve-ment of a simple life unconcerned with who the oracle is and where it originated is nothing less than the truth itself.

The story of Theuth and Thamus concerns writing, but it is also about simplicity. One of the faults Socrates sees in writing is its solemn and perennial silence. A written text cannot speak for itself; it roams eternally, going from hand to hand, from learned readers to ignorant, all of them making it say something, anything. A written text 'always needs its father's support; alone, it can neither defend itself nor come to its own support.'[6] A text, feeble and co-dependent, amounts to a collection of words with no life of their own, and yet passing for true knowledge, calligraphed on a papyrus that will inevitably disintegrate over time. A written text is constrained by its own materiality. A good speech, on the other hand, delivered by a capable speaker, imprints itself on the soul of the listener. It lives freely and indelibly.[7] An effective speech is the 'living discourse of the man who knows, of which the written one can be fairly called an image'.[8] For Socrates, the skilled speaker chooses 'a proper soul and plants and sows within it discourse accompanied by knowledge'.[9] He must sow the type of discourse that will flourish and self-seed year after year. He must be knowledgeable; he must define the parts of his discourse and divide each one until they are no longer divisible – in other words, until they are simple. He must adapt his discourse to his audience and deliver only a simple speech to simple souls.[10] This, for Socrates, is best achieved in the copresence of both the locutor and the interlocutor; it can also be conveyed, although not as perfectly, in writing. But even when the simplification of subject and style is achieved in writing, the immediacy and intimacy of direct communication are still lacking from the once-removed relationship of writer to writing to reader. True simplicity is unmediated; its reward: to hear the true messages sounded by trees, wind and people. And yet, it is the written word that will continue to bear fruit – some poisonous, some curative – year after year, long after the tree has returned to the ground and stopped talking. Writing is a potion or *pharmakon*; it is a healing poison and a poisonous remedy. For Jacques Derrida, the *pharmakon* 'does not have the punctual simplicity of a *coincidentia oppositorum*'; in other words, it cannot be reduced to a set of binaries.[11] The *pharmakon* is ambivalent:

> The 'essence' of the *pharmakon* lies in the way in which, having no stable essence, no 'proper' characteristics, it is not, in any sense (metaphysical, physical, chemical, alchemical) of the word, a *substance*. The *pharmakon* has no ideal identity; it is aneidetic, firstly because it is not monoeidetic (in the sense in which the *Phaedo* speaks of the *eidos* as something simple, noncomposite: *monoeides*). This 'medicine' is not a simple thing. But neither is it a composite, a sensible or empirical *suntheton* partaking of several simple essences.[12]

The *pharmakon* is not simple in that it is not reducible to one entity, nor is it the synthesis of several singular entities. It is not a mere concoction of remedial and poisonous elements; it is, as Derrida suggests, 'the prior medium in which differentiation in general is produced, along with the opposition between the *eidos* and its other'.[13] The *pharmakon* is an energy, or a 'medium', that brings into being *différance*, where meaning is always differed and reinforced by differences, or binary oppositions. It is also a supplement that disrupts the integrity of a simple entity even if it was administered to cure it; it is an addition to that which was whole, a mixture causing the modification of an essence.[14] *Pharmakon* in Greek also refers to a dye, an alteration of a natural colour. On the shield of Aphelia, goddess of simplicity, Ben Jonson wrote 'omnis abest fucus', 'all is without colour', without dissimulation or deceit.[15] The goddess lent her name to a type of simple discourse that emulates the unrefined spontaneity of speech, best represented by Xenophon of Ephesus (*fl.* second–third century CE).[16] Simplicity evokes achromatic, unmodified and pure states, contrasting at first glance with the buoyant indeterminacy of the *pharmakon*. But simplicity and the *pharmakon* cannot be neatly severed without creating false binaries, resulting in reductionist associations and images: *pharmakon* as generative, unruly and expansive energy, on the one hand; on the other, simplicity as voluntary renunciation of excess for the passive but immediate apprehension of knowledge.

Pre-Socratic philosophers situated the principles of all things in one or more fundamental elements that were not affected by the coming into being or modification of things. For Thales, water is the original and universal substance from which everything arises and returns; this original substance is never destroyed, just modified.[17] 'Anaximenes and Diogenes', Aristotle reports, 'make air prior to water, and the most primary of simple bodies.'[18] The simplicity of bodies, air being the simplest, refers to its eternal conservation. Empedocles has the four elements – water, fire, air and earth – as the origin of all that exists; these elements, says Aristotle, 'always remain and do not come to be, except that they come to be more or fewer, being aggregated into one and segregated out of one.'[19] Simple elements are defined by their self-conservation and their regenerative qualities. Parmenides, the so-called 'Father of Metaphysics', introduced the idea that there is just one thing in the world and that this thing is 'uncreated and indestructible; for it is complete, immovable, and without end'.[20] Simplicity as conservation and the Parmenidean idea of Oneness of reality or 'what is' infuse later philosophies. In Plato's *Theaetetus*, Socrates presents Parmenides as a philosopher who 'insist[s] that all things are One, and that this One stands still, itself within itself, having no place in which to move'.[21] Socrates will concede later in the dialogue that such ideas as those of Parmenides on simplicity and Oneness are immensely complex and may not be treated lightly.[22]

In *Phaedo*, Socrates introduces the idea of Forms as *mono-eides*, or uniform. According to the Theory of Forms, Forms are the reason why things are what they are. Something is beautiful because it participates in the Form of Beauty. 'It is through Beauty that beautiful things are made beautiful', not because of their colour or shape.[23] Here Plato is sketching out what came to be known as the 'two-world theory'. In the world of Forms, Forms are single, unchangeable, of their essence, intelligible, invisible to the eye but accessible by the mind.[24] On the contrary, the world of particulars that we inhabit is unintelligible but perceivable: it is made of composite, multiform, changing and passing things.[25] Though Plato revisited and challenged the Theory of Forms in his dialogue *Parmenides*, the idea that Forms are simple and constitute the highest degree of good will be conserved, although modified, in Plotinus.

At the core of the philosophy of the Neoplatonist Plotinus resides the One. The One eludes attempts to be captured by reason and language, yet its *dunamis* or dynamic emanation can be experienced in contemplation or vision: the One is the possibility of existence. As it expands, the One generates Intelligence, or *Nous*.

It is precisely because there is nothing within the One that all things are from it: in order that Being may be brought about, the source must be no Being but Being's generator, in what is to be thought of as the primal act of generation. Seeking nothing, possessing nothing, lacking nothing, the One is perfect and, in our metaphor, has overflowed, and its exuberance has produced the new: this product has turned again to its begetter and been filled and has become its contemplator and so an Intellectual-Principle.[26]

The emanation of the other, or *Nous*, is not a modification of the One, which is unchangeable and always present to Itself. The *Nous* is the One seeing Itself present in the pure energy of its emanation. The *Nous* or Intelligence has the capacity to see the One from which it receives its unity and the capacity to see its own thoughts. For the *Nous*, thinking and being are the same. The totality of thoughts is assimilated by Plotinus to the totality of Plato's Forms. In Plotinian philosophy, the first principle is then the *Nous*, which is both one and capable of generation and multiplicity. The *Nous* is also called God or *Theos*. One aspect of Plotinus' philosophy and of Neoplatonism that is of interest to a reflection on simplicity is the logical and permanent relation between the original emanation whence the *Nous* emanates and the Soul, which emanates from the *Nous*. In the ninth tractate of the second book of the *Enneads*, Plotinus posits that the One, also called the Good, is simplex and therefore primal, and that 'it is an integral Unity.'[27] *Simplex* means self-sufficing (or not dependent on any other constituents), not compound, self-contained and containing nothing. 'Deriving then from nothing alien, entering into nothing alien, in no way a made-up thing, there can be nothing above it.'[28]

Plotinus admits that there are entities that are more simplex than others but there is nothing more simplex than the One. Then the simplex One begot God (Intelligence or *Nous*), meaning that Simplex or Unity precedes God. Is the simplex One knowable? The One is not knowable because 'in knowing, soul or mind abandons its unity; it cannot remain a simplex: knowing is taking account of things; that accounting is multiple; the mind thus plunging into number and multiplicity departs from unity.'[29] Such emanations can be experienced in *Henosis* or state of oneness with the One. *Henosis* is possible when we 'withdraw from all the extern, pointed wholly inwards'.[30] At the end of the *Enneads*, Plotinus elucidates the question: 'There were not two; beholder was one with beheld; it was not a vision compassed but a unity apprehended.'[31] Plotinus describes the isolation, stillness and rest, or rather the becoming isolation, the becoming still and the becoming rest. This, continues Plotinus, 'was scarcely vision, unless of a mode unknown; it was a going forth from the self, a simplifying, a renunciation, a reach towards contact and at the same time a repose, a meditation towards adjustment.'[32]

The *Enneads* conclude with a description of the ascent of the soul:

It is not in the soul's nature to touch utter nothingness; the lowest descent is into evil, and, so far, into non-being: but to utter nothing, never. When the soul begins again to mount, it comes not to something alien but to its very self; thus detached, it is in nothing but itself; self-gathered it is no longer in the order of being; it is in the Supreme.[33]

The process of simplifying (self-detachment and self-gathering) in the *Henosis*, although unaccountable by the one who experiences it because it is beyond words, and beyond being, culminates in the unity with the simplex One.

In a direct address to the reader and in an attempt to dispel any confusion concerning his intentions, Plotinus states his mission in the second book of the *Enneads*: 'I leave it to yourselves to read the books and examine the rest of the doctrine: you will note all through how our form of philosophy inculcates simplicity of character and honest thinking in addition to all other good qualities.'[34] The *Enneads*, according to its author, is a bold but reasonable text, in which ideas progress with caution and circumspection and are supported by 'careful proof'.[35] Methodical thinking is at the service of a specific goal: to teach simplicity of mind and action.

Teaching is the vital nerve of ancient philosophy. Socrates was the teacher of Plato, who was the teacher of Aristotle. The acquisition of abstract knowledge was not the aim of philosophical teaching. Rather, teaching aimed at changing, even at converting, students. Blaise Pascal captured what was philosophical about philosophy:

> We can only imagine Plato and Aristotle in long academic gowns. They were honest men like others, laughing with their friends. And when they amused themselves with their *Laws* and their *Politics*, they did it as a game. This was the least philosophic and least serious part of their life, the most philosophic being living simply and quietly.[36]

Philosophy amounted to more than games of the intellect; it was a way of life, as the works of Pierre Hadot and others before him have shown us.[37] Pascal was right to redirect our attention to philosophy as a way of life, as a way for a simpler life, although some philosophers, like Nietzsche, will concede that 'the simple life is ... too lofty a goal, and better left to the wisest.'[38] For Nietzsche, the 'simplest' of philosophers was Socrates.[39]

Xenophon, a lesser known student of Socrates, wrote in defence of his teacher, who was accused of introducing new gods to the city, of refusing to recognize the gods of the state religion and of corrupting the young. His apology of Socrates is found in his *Memorabilia*. In it, Xenophon narrates a series of encounters between the alleged father of philosophy and a variety of interlocutors. One such encounter reads:

Socrates, I supposed that philosophy must add to one's store of happiness. But the fruits you have reaped from philosophy are apparently very different. For example, you are living a life that would drive even a slave to desert his master. Your meat and drink are of the poorest: the cloak you wear is not only a poor thing, but it is never changed summer or winter; and you never wear shoes or tunic. Besides you refuse to take money, the mere getting of which is a joy, while its possession makes one more independent and happier. Now the professors of other subjects try to make their pupils copy their teachers: if you intend to make your companions do that, you must consider yourself a professor of unhappiness.[40]

Those are the words of Antiphon the Sophist describing Socrates. The portrait painted here is a far cry from the usual images of the venerable old philosopher who sacrificed his life for truth.

Antiphon's intention in this passage was to draw his companions away from Socrates by showing them that his brand of philosophy does not beget happiness. His argument against Socrates was that philosophy should not be a lesson in the paucity of means, the abnegation of pleasure and distrust in such conventions as money. For the Sophist, to profess such simplicity of means, desires and needs meant to profess the opposite of philosophy and happiness. Socrates' response, as reported by Xenophon, reads: 'You seem, Antiphon, to imagine that happiness consists in luxury and extravagance. But my belief is that to have no wants is divine; to have as few as possible comes next to the divine . . .'[41]

The frugality and restraint that Socrates professes are achieved by way of self-control, as we would call it today, a form of control over the passions that is directly related to self-knowledge. The only commerce Socrates engages in is that of ideas and friends:

> my fancy . . . is for good friends. I teach them all the good
> I can, and recommend them to others from whom I think
> they will get some moral benefit. And the treasures that
> the wise men of old have left us in their writings I open
> and explore with my friends. If we come on any good
> thing, we extract it, and we set much store on being useful
> to one another.[42]

Socrates' riches are his friends, his students, people he does not claim for himself. His riches are also the writings of others, which he mines for ideas useful for all and shared by all. The intellectual communalism advocated here clashes with the Sophist's idea of proprietary luxuries. And Xenophon would confirm that Socrates was indeed a happy man himself who lived by his word, simply.[43]

The main philosophical schools that emerged from Socratism all embrace simplicity in one form or another as a means to regulate one's desires, needs and inclinations. For those who prefer material abundance and luxury, simplicity acts as a moral corset of a sort that chokes their very existence. For others, simplicity is the requisite for physical, mental and moral health, which ultimately contributes to healthier and more just societies.

In Book VI of the *Republic*, Plato draws the portrait of the philosopher-king: 'Then surely such a person is moderate and not at all a money-lover. It's appropriate for others to take seriously the things for which money and large expenditures are needed, but not for him.'[44] The philosopher is the one who sees beyond appearances and who moderates his passions by way of reason. He is a man fit to rule. Likewise, the lives of the guardians – the city rulers and soldiers – are not lives of luxury and excess but of simplicity:

First, none of them should possess any private property beyond what is wholly necessary. Second, none of them should have a house or storeroom that isn't open for all to enter at will. Third, whatever sustenance moderate and courageous warrior-athletes require in order to have neither shortfall nor surplus in a given year they'll receive by taxation on the other citizens as a salary for their guardianship. Fourth, they'll have common messes and live together like soldiers in a camp. We'll tell them that they always have gold and silver of a divine sort in their souls as a gift from the gods and so have no further need of human gold.[45]

In the *Republic*, Plato advises that the ruling class lead a communal life, as private property, wealth or family jeopardize the unity and concord of the city and of those who govern it. Should the guardians of the city engage in private ownership or possession of human gold or money, they will live the lives of mere household managers or farmers. Their energy will be spent hating others and fearing internal foes and plotters more than foreign enemies. Eventually, they will destroy their own lives and ruin the city. Other members of the city as devised by Socrates will also lead simple lives:

> They'll produce bread, wine, clothes, and shoes, won't they? They'll build houses, work naked and barefoot in the summer, and wear adequate clothing and shoes in the winter. For food, they'll knead and cook the flour and meal they've made from wheat and barley. They'll put their honest cakes and loaves on reeds or clean leaves, and, reclining on beds strewn with yew and myrtle, they'll feast with their children, drink their wine, and, crowned with wreaths, hymn the gods. They'll enjoy sex with one another but bear no more children than their resources allow, lest they fall into either poverty or war . . .
>
> . . . they'll obviously need salt, olives, cheese, boiled roots, and vegetables of the sort they cook in the country. We'll give them desserts, too, of course, consisting of figs, chickpeas, and beans, and they'll roast myrtle and acorns before the fire, drinking moderately. And so they'll live in peace and good health, and when they die at a ripe old age, they'll bequeath a similar life to their children.[46]

This is the city of simplicity where any form of superfluity is banned; where peace, concord and happiness prosper; where the future is as certain and predictable as the present is at the service of justice. For these simple ways of life are inseparable from their *telos* or end: justice.

Glaucon, Socrates' interlocutor and contradictor, paints the portrait of the just man who is 'simple and noble and who . . . doesn't want to be believed to be good but to be so'.[47] So that the just man may not seek the rewards that a reputation of justness may bring him, he imagines that he is falsely accused of injustice. Perceived as an unjust man, he will suffer extreme punishment and even torture. With this thought experiment, Glaucon is asking Socrates whether justice is good in itself, or whether we are drawn to it for its rewards, or because of the fear of punishment it may instil in us. As Socrates demonstrates, justice is more than merely legislation, regulations and a set of prescribed behaviours. Indeed, justice can be observed in the city-state and in the individual, and both types of justice, societal and personal, are structurally similar. Does this mean that all people who live in a just city will be just? According to Socrates, there is no causal relation. A just person may not feel compelled to abide by all the laws of a just city and a just city may not be inhabited by just people only. Nonetheless, the just city, in its ideal form, is characterized by four traits, which translate to the four cardinal virtues of its citizens. The city and her people are 'wise, courageous, moderate, and just'.[48] Wisdom or intellectual virtue is the basis of the other three. 'But you meet with the desires that are simple, measured, and directed by calculation in accordance with understanding and correct belief only in the few people who are born with the best natures and receive the best education,' wrote Plato.[49] The ideal and just city, the city where courage and wisdom dictate behaviour and decisions – this city is ruled by an intellectual aristocracy comprised of men blessed by natural intelligence, honour and the determination perfected by education. The difference between wisdom, courage and moderation is that the last extends beyond the circle of the ruling class. All citizens regardless of means and situations are united in the virtue of moderation. And it is with moderation that they all come to an agreement, among themselves and as a group, about who should rule. Moderation is both a social and a moral equalizer as well as a simple, genuine, artless process of political selection. While justice is the *telos* of the civic life, simplicity and moderation serve as bonding agents among all citizens. The just city is one where simple, moderate rulers rule over simple, moderate people.

Plato's student, Aristotle, has a different view on frugality and simplicity. He defines the happy man as one who lives a life in conformity with complete virtue and who is 'sufficiently equipped with external goods, not for some chance period but throughout a complete life'.[50] Happiness, the highest good of the soul, derives from virtuous activity. Other goods such as health, wealth and power are not constitutive of the highest good but may contribute to it if employed moderately and appropriately. A certain amount of external goods (wealth, friends and power, for instance) is necessary for most virtuous acts, plus such goods can make our lives 'blessed' while adding beauty to them.[51] Too many or too few external goods, particularly wealth, will impact one's happiness negatively. Aristotle outlines four ways to acquire external goods or wealth: one, directly from nature; two, bartering; three, monetary exchanges; and four, trade, banking or wage labour. A type of acquisition is good if it contributes to virtuous activities for the household, the state, or ideally for both. The *telos* of this type of natural acquisition is virtue. Unnatural acquisition of wealth will have no other end but the thirst to acquire more, which is endless. Wealth as provided directly by nature, whose role it is to satisfy human needs, is natural and good. Conversely, trading natural resources for the sole purpose of increasing the trader's wealth is unnatural. Trading to increase one's capital is trading one's personal excellence or virtue – the prerequisite for the good life – for a life of slavishness and poor health. The worst type of wealth acquisition is usury, for it 'makes a gain out of money itself, and not from the natural object of it'.[52]

Aristotle's position on private possessions differs from Plato's communism on several grounds, most notably on the question of care. 'For that which is common to the greatest number has the least care bestowed upon it,' writes Aristotle in the *Politics*.[53] If laws can make citizens virtuous, then virtues such as generosity will promote the sharing of private possessions and their common use. In situations of communal ownership as advocated by Plato, generosity does not spring naturally. Why would I want to share something with someone if everything is owned communally? In such a situation, I cannot even experience the pleasure of generosity. The common use of privately owned objects will depend on the generosity of the owner; it is not a right extended to all members of the community. It is an act of virtue which authorizes common use. Granting the use of one's property is a virtuous expression of the individual will.[54] Willed generosity, Aristotle believes, can be nurtured and habituated by education if teaching is placed under the aegis of legislators. Of course, this may be asking a lot of education, the Law and habituation, but for Aristotle, living a simple life was a reality at hand for the individual and the families willing it, and a simple life was for him the way towards excellence and self-fulfilment. Such a life gives you the opportunity to do good and be good, and ultimately to fulfil your highest potential.

Simplicity, frugality and moderation play a part in the philosophical dialogues and teachings of ancient Greek philosophers. As shown in these examples from Plato and Aristotle, simplicity is also a matter of state, and of politics. While songs of simplicity can still be heard in political arenas today, as we will see later, it is hard to imagine that our guardians, if they can be called that, would renounce private possessions and fame to adopt simpler ways of life. Private property is rarely seen as an opportunity to share and experience the pleasure of generosity. Communalism is relegated to intentional communities, or to the past, and has rapidly become conflated with failed historical attempts at communism, loosely defined. Most of all, simplicity seems to be absent from political discourse. When it appears at all, it appears in a perilous form called simplism. Current elected and electing members of our society give us daily examples of simplism. But this was not always the case. One philosopher and Roman emperor did embrace simplicity as a way of life and as a way of governing. His name was Marcus Aurelius, a Stoic at heart, in mind and in public affairs.

Simplicity, for Stoic philosophers, was not an end in itself but rather a means towards a greater self-knowledge and happiness, understood as the good life or *eudaimonia*. The good life is not a fleeting moment of delight but a long-term fulfilment resulting from the practice of moderation and virtue. Stoicism shares a few traits with Epicureanism. While the two philosophical schools differed in their definitions of what constitutes the good life and the practice of it, both teach the surveillance of passions, desires, whether natural, unnatural, or empty, to use the Epicurean classification, so that passions may not inconspicuously impose their dominion on unprepared, unaware souls. While the exercises prescribed by these schools aimed at moderation in all matters, they did not have simplicity as a core virtue but as a regulatory means, with perhaps the notable exception of Marcus Aurelius. His *Meditations* are possibly the most popular work of Graeco-Roman philosophy today. As a Stoic, Marcus Aurelius advocated self-discipline and the regulation of the passions or *pathê*, which control you if left unattended. Self-discipline is not a set of constraining principles or rules but emancipatory exercises that free us from the imperiousness of the passions. Self-discipline is coupled with careful and permanent attention to the soundness of one's judgement, which should be aligned with reason, a universal principle shared by gods and humans. Stoics did not advocate for the complete renunciation of all material goods, but for their reasonable and measured use, so they may not gain control of the person. Possibly more than for any other philosophical school of the ancient world, freedom is the pulse of Stoicism.

Marcus Aurelius' *Meditations* is not a Stoic treatise but a collection of notes to himself on how to live a good life. The overall intention of the emperor's fragmentary thoughts was less dogmatic than analytical and self-reflective. Knowing oneself starts with knowing one's lineage. He recalls that he inherited the integrity and strength of character of his father and grandfather. He admired his mother for her 'simple way – not in the least like the rich'.[55] In the succinct portrait of his mother, Marcus Aurelius uses the Greek word λιτόν, which is translated by Gregory Hays as 'simple'. Translation is dictated by precision but also by historical and cultural contexts. For instance, the Greek ἁπλῶς is rendered by Hays as 'straightforward', while Francis Hutcheson and James Moor, who translated the *Meditations* in the eighteenth century, preferred the adjective 'simple'. *Haplôs*, the transliteration of ἁπλῶς, spans a range of adjacent meanings related to the idea of singleness of spirit, rectitude and univocity. In Chapter Fifteen of Book XI of the *Meditations*, Marcus Aurelius reflects on ἁπλότης or *haplotês*. This is how Hays translates it:

> The despicable phoniness of people who say, 'Listen, I'm going to level with you here.' What does that mean? It shouldn't even need to be said. It should be obvious – written in block letters on your forehead. It should be audible in your voice, visible in your eyes, like a lover who looks into your face and takes in the whole story at a glance. A straightforward, honest person should be like someone who stinks: when you're in the same room with him, you know it. But false straightforwardness is like a knife in the back.
>
> False friendship is the worst. Avoid it at all costs. If you're honest and straightforward and mean well, it should show in your eyes. It should be unmistakable.[56]

For Marcus Aurelius, simplicity or straightforwardness needs to be externalized – impressed on and expressed by the body – here by the eyes. Simplicity or straightforwardness is more than a character trait; it is an ability to convey virtue unequivocally and in so doing act virtuously. This is particularly important for the Stoics, as perception is central to their philosophy and way of life. It is not the thing you perceive that leads you astray; it is the perception you have that may distort the thing itself. An improper perception may be doubly compounded by an erroneous interpretation of the thing or event. In most cases, the interpretation of what happened, which is always supplementary to the event itself, is unnecessary and potentially an obstacle to the peace and goodness of your life. Stoicism teaches you how to perceive simply so that you are able to distinguish between what is and what is interpreted. The above passage from the *Meditations* also conveys the importance of economy of expression. An expression should not be ambiguous but obvious, so that a 'whole story' may be taken in at once, or 'at a glance'. The simpler the message, the less interpretation and fewer opportunities for errors it may generate. Friendship is a case in point. Communication with another human being and especially a friend – whether verbal, olfactory or ocular, to use examples from the quoted meditation – should leave no room for mistake or the relationship may become riddled with faults and tension. Simplicity is a communication and an interpersonal imperative. False simplicity is a mortal vice, a 'knife in the back'. False simplicity, in Stoic ethics, is an intention or action that also harms the one who commits it. True simplicity or straightforwardness is a virtue that contributes to the good life of the straightforward, simple philosopher-emperor.

Marcus Aurelius has long been associated with Stoicism, and for good reason, but his education exposed him to a wide range of philosophies and philosophers, including a certain group of independent thinkers and libertines whom he mentions in one of his meditations:

Like seeing roasted meat and other dishes in front of you and suddenly realizing: This is a dead fish. A dead bird.

A dead pig. Or that this noble vintage is grape juice, and the purple robes are sheep wool dyed with shellfish blood. Or making love – something rubbing against your penis, a brief seizure and a little cloudy liquid.

Perceptions like that – latching onto things and piercing through them, so we see what they really are. That's what we need to do all the time – to lay them bare and see how pointless they are, to strip away the legend that encrusts them.

Pride is a master of deception: when you think you're occupied in the weightiest business, that's when he has you in his spell.

(Compare Crates on Xenocrates).[57]

Crates, mentioned in the parenthetical remark, was a well-known Cynic philosopher who was the teacher of Zeno of Citium, the founder of Stoicism. This meditation concerns perception; like the meditation cited above it is about naming things simply. Let's call a pig a pig, and not pork, even after it has been slaughtered and dressed up, Marcus Aurelius recommends. Without fermentation, wine is just grape juice. Purple, the colour exclusive to magistrates, consuls and the emperor, is extracted from the mucus of a sea-snail. Making love is merely friction that provokes the expression of body fluids. Marcus Aurelius is doing more than just calling a spade a spade; he is stripping words of the supplementary symbolic and conventional values that create a distance between the thing and the word. Unnecessary symbolism, euphemistic words like pork and also those processes that denature, as Rousseau will say much later, such as fermentation and dyeing, are exposed and disposed of. Straightforwardness and simplicity trace the short line between a word and what it represents. Processes that change the raw material and symbols that coat a word invite interpretations and errors. The Stoics and Cynics share the view that, when it comes to language, the simpler the better. In many other ways, they differ.

Living according to nature is the goal of Stoicism. This notion has fuelled many different interpretations and disagreements. Suffice it to say that for the Stoics all events, processes, changes and systems that compose the universe and the natural world are part of an organized scheme called *Logos*. Living according to nature means, in this case, living in accord with the sequence of events that make the world what it is. But living according to nature can also mean to live according to one's own nature: in your case and mine, according to our human nature. What defines human nature for the Stoics is reason. Living according to reason is living according to nature, human nature. Let's not pretend to draw conclusions here on this difficult issue, but let's mention that we might succumb to over-interpretation if we believed that the Stoics were precursors of any return-to-nature impulses or philosophy. The same can be said of the Cynics.

The Cynics, including Crates, who is mentioned in Marcus Aurelius' meditation above, embraced a similar creed. Living according to nature was central to their philosophy. But for them it meant adopting a way of life many Stoics would have condemned. Unlike the Stoic philosophers, the Cynics did not elaborate a philosophy of nature based on observations of the cosmos, the earth and its non-human habitants. Rather, they saw nature as what is at hand or present. Dio Chrysostom, in his discourse entitled 'Diogenes, or on Tyranny', borrows a Cynic argument to demonstrate that man has no need for luxuries such as lavish clothing or extravagant dishes. When Diogenes was shivering outside in the cold, he was in fact strengthening his body against the ills that afflict those who do not step outside as winter rolls in. Diogenes needed only one garment; he wore no shoes. He drank from a stream as animals do and only when he was thirsty, unlike those who drink expensive wines even when they do not need to. A nomadic life solved seasonal difficulties, as migrating animals know instinctively. Nature becomes a florilegium of virtues and ingenuities that leads to the conclusion that what all animals can do, man also can do. 'Else how could the first human beings to be born have survived, there being no fire, or houses, or clothing, or any other food than that which grew wild?'[58] Man's ingenuity turned against him as his inventions set him at a remove from his natural needs and the bounty of nature. Man's ingenuity is spent in devising instruments of pleasure rather than fostering courage and justice. An anecdote reported by Diogenes Laërtius captures the practical and natural spirit of Cynicism and of Diogenes of Sinope in particular. 'One day,' reports the Greek biographer, 'observing a child drinking out of his hands, Diogenes cast away the cup from his wallet with the words, "A child has beaten me in plainness of living".'[59] The Cynics were keen observers of the natural world of which man is but a single part. They learnt from what they saw. Mainly, they learnt how to dispose of excess, of unnatural artefacts and unnecessary practices and to imitate the simple effectiveness of nature and children. The simplicity found in nature or in those uncorrupted by convention and false needs prompted the Cynics to reflect upon themselves. Nature becomes a norm or standard for determining what is excessive and what is just enough or unadulterated.

No Cynic text has survived. Their ideas have come down to us at second hand in the form of portraits of the eccentrics who refused to observe the laws of the land, preferring instead the fortuitousness of nature. Did Diogenes of Sinope not live in a *pithos*, even in the summer heat? Didn't he live like a dog, eating and drinking in public? Didn't he have such a disregard for moral laws that he masturbated in public places when nature called? But Cynic ethics are more than a litany of eccentricities; what Cynics did, they did for a reason. Living like a dog in the public eye was a public renunciation of societal conventions and mores. Living a meagre existence, facing hardships as they arose, was part of a Cynic practice called *ponos* ('toil' or 'labour'), enduring nature in whatever way or form she manifests herself in the moment. Simple desires can easily be satisfied *in situ* and in the moment if one pays no heed to conventions, remaining blind to the gaze of the other. Living simply in the present and with only what is at hand is the condition for virtue. With such simple needs as those dictated by the moment, who needs to wage wars, invade other countries or commit crimes?[60] Liberated from the fetters of societal constraints and unnatural needs, the Cynic is a free man or woman. This freedom is expressed in their self-sufficiency and in free speech, or *parrhēsia*, which is also more than just calling a spade a spade: it means disrespecting rank in direct address; it means also telling the truth under all circumstances. Living according to the law of the moment and embracing freedom in all one's actions and expressions made the Cynic stand out in a crowd of well-behaved citizens. It is well known that when asked where he was from, Diogenes of Sinope replied: 'I am a citizen of the world,' a *kosmopolitēs*. His city is not Sinope; the laws he abides by are not Sinopean. Diogenes belongs to the cosmos, that which is greater than Sinope or any other city-state. He is a free man unconstrained by the laws of one city. His only law: nature or the cosmos as it happens.

About Cynicism, the emperor Julian wrote: 'There were always men who practiced this philosophy. For it seems to be in some ways a universal philosophy, and the most natural.'[61] The legacy of Cynicism is varied. Beyond Stoicism, Cynic ethics permeated Christianity and Enlightenment philosophies. In his illustration of frugality and renunciation in *Against Jovinianus*, St Jerome praises the Cynics, Antisthenes, Diogenes of Sinope and Crates, who forsake his considerable fortune when he adopted the Cynic way of life. Diogenes, writes Jerome, 'was mightier than King Alexander in that he conquered human nature.'[62] The philosopher, according to Jerome, embodies 'Gentile moderation.'[63] The Church Fathers decried the bawdiness of Cynic ways and especially their public displays of sexuality, but some Christian theologians saw a lesson to follow in the simplicity Cynics had determined as a way of life. Cynic austerity was hailed also as a virtue to be emulated by those who had decided to embrace an ascetic life.

No absolute equivalence should be drawn between those whose lives were ruled by self-sufficiency, freedom of speech and shamelessness and those who embraced a life dedicated to Christ. Tales of Cynics' simple lives were often contrasted to the higher forms of simplicity practised by Christians. In the early modern world, simplicity was primarily hailed as a very Christian virtue. Cynics were also often mocked, and their name used to insult sects whose ways were not in accord with those of the Church. In the early eighteenth century, when histories and dictionaries started to fill up bookshelves, one André-François Boureau-Deslandes published a critical history of philosophy. His intention in his *Histoire* was not to recreate a chronicle of philosophers or philosophies but to show that to think well is to live well. In the second volume, Boureau-Deslandes dedicated a number of pages to Cynicism. He first lists all the crimes against common values and morality committed by ancient Cynics, like Crates throwing away his fortune in the sea or the many accounts of fornication in public. He argues against the Cynics' view that laws are conventional and arbitrary. But Boureau-Deslandes reminds his reader that amoral actions do not necessarily exclude purity and the ordering of sentiments and intentions. Once this is established, the eighteenth century can praise the Cynics for their independence of spirit and body, for their disregard of money, and even for their indifference to insults against their opinions and lives. Nothing could make them falter, writes Boureau-Deslandes.[64] He praises Diogenes for preferring his *pithos* to a palace. The Cynic had to live because he was born; he lived neither fearing death nor fearing life.[65] He mentions the commonalities between monks and Cynics before tracing the legacy of Diogenes in the Christian era. According to Boureau-Deslandes traces of Cynicism are found in the following Christian sects: Ebionites, Manicheans, Adamites, Beghards, Turlupins, Waldenses, Flagellants, Humiliati, Cathars, Paterins, Anabaptists, Mennonites, Quakers and the French Prophets. All these sectarians, according to Boureau-Deslandes, are Christian Cynics.[66] All lived on the margins of orthodoxy. Some advocated and practised nudity (Adamites and Turlupins), some preached voluntary poverty (Ebionites, Beghards), some professed universalism (French Prophets) and others spoke in plain speech as the Cynics did (Quakers). All practised simplicity. Before turning to these alleged neo-Cynics who believed in the Christian God, let us investigate the lives of those who embraced a Christian life fully clothed, and in all simplicity.

TWO

WALKING IN SIMPLICITY

There was a man in the land of Uz, whose name was Job; and
that man was perfect and upright, and one that feared God, and
eschewed evil.

Job 1:1[1]

In the Old Testament, Job exemplifies simplicity and unvan-
quished faith in God's decrees. 'Perfection' and 'uprightness',
his foremost moral qualities, are translated from *simplex* and *rectus*
in the Latin text of the Vulgate. The original Hebrew for *simplex*
suggests wholeness and perfection in oneself: Job's uprightness
also evokes his perfection, but a relative perfection defined in
comparison to others.[2] Job is 'simple' because he is perfect in
himself; he is just because he obeys the justice of God. Simple
and upright, Job lost everything and yet never questioned divine
justice. Unlike other books of the Scriptures, the Book of Job
does not promulgate observances and rituals; it concerns the
life of a faithful man who accepted true justice and preserved
his spiritual and physical integrity by living a simple life. Here,
simplicity is paired with perfection and justice; it also conveys
the pure intention to walk the path of righteousness to the end.

The greatest example of simple moral rectitude, intention and martyrdom appears in the First Book of Maccabees when, on the Sabbath, the troops of Antiochus IV attacked a group of rebel Jews who had fled to the wilderness to live according to Hebraic Law. 'We will all die in our simplicity,' shouted the defiant Jews, who gathered in a cave, braving the enemy with the courage of religious conviction.[3] They refused to fight on the Sabbath. Their exemplary deaths testified that as simple and just observants they never disobeyed their one God. Their simplicity was one of singularity of intention and strict obedience, a willingness to obey a force greater than themselves, which commanded their souls, actions and words. Dying in all simplicity is the lot of the martyr who dies in accord with himself, his faith and his God. In his death, the martyr finds the ultimate wholeness or simplicity. However, the deaths of the men and women under the sword of Antiochus convinced their leader, Mattathias, that to save lives the Law could be broken on the Sabbath. Renunciation and martyrdom do not always rhyme with simplicity. Many saints lived long, simple lives and died peaceful deaths, as did many more ordinary men and women of unwavering faith who embraced simplicity as a way of life.

In the Catechism of the Catholic Church, simplicity is neither one of the four cardinal virtues nor one of the three theological virtues; it nevertheless occupies a prominent place in Christian ethics. In the canonical Scriptures and in the apocryphal literature, simplicity intersects with a wide range of virtues, such as humility, integrity, obedience, innocence, rectitude and good faith. The adjective 'simple' commonly describes a heart that exhibits these virtues. Above all, a simple heart is generous. It gives liberally, and it is big. Only the big-hearted are simple.

I know also, my God, that thou triest the heart, and hast pleasure in uprightness [*simplicitatem*]. As for me, in the uprightness of my heart [*simplicitate cordis*] I have willingly offered all these things: and now have I seen with joy thy people, which are present here, to offer willingly unto thee.[4]

God loves simplicity, uprightness and justice. The question raised by David in First Chronicles is about the nature of giving, not of God's gifts to man but of man's gifts to God. How can we give to God when He is the one who has given us everything in the first place? Is giving just 'giving back'? A simple heart does not care about what is given nor is it concerned with how something is given. A simple heart gives willingly and with joy. When it gives, it does nothing else but give. A simple heart wills giving; and in return, the will and the joy make the heart simpler. Giving in simplicity is explained by St Paul. In Romans 12:6–8, Paul presses us to 'think soberly' of ourselves according to the gifts given to us by grace:

> Having then gifts differing according to the grace that is given to us, whether prophecy, *let us prophesy* according to the proportion of faith; or ministry, *let us wait* on *our* ministering: or he that teacheth, on teaching; or he that exhorteth, on exhortation: he that giveth, *let him do it* with simplicity [*in simplicitate*]; he that ruleth, with diligence; he that sheweth mercy, with cheerfulness.[5]

The Latin of the Vulgate, *in simplicitate*, could be translated as 'generously', but in the context of Romans 12, simplicity is less a manner of giving than an attribute of giving. A giving, simple heart is a heart that clings to nothing because it owns nothing. The gift of the giver disowns him of everything, so he can simply give. To simply give is to do nothing but give while giving nothing. He that giveth, giveth because he has the gift of giving in simplicity.

The Wisdom of Solomon, or Book of Solomon, was originally written in Greek, admittedly by a single author who was knowledgeable in Greek philosophy. It opens with an address to rulers:

> Love righteousness, ye that be judges: think [*sentite*] of the Lord with a good [heart], and in simplicity of heart seek him. For he will be found of them that tempt him not; and sheweth himself unto such as do not distrust him.[6]

The exhortation makes a distinction between the good heart and the simple heart. While both evoke goodness and purity of intention, the latter is associated with a search, and thus an absence, rather than an experience, be it a rational or a sensory experience, as both meanings are present in the Latin *sentite*. The good heart experiences; the simple heart searches. The seeking heart is capable of seeing within the absence the possibility of revelation; in its simplicity, it sees in the absence the possibility of presence. The simple heart does not distinguish or differentiate between what is and what is not; that is the role of the good heart. Nor does the simple heart unite, because for it nothing is disunited, and everything is one.

In the margins of ecclesiastical history lie a body of texts that shed light on the ideas of simple living in early Christianity. Of particular interest is the Testament of Issachar Concerning

Simplicity, one of the twelve apocryphal texts comprising the Testaments of the Twelve Patriarchs or the Twelve Sons of Jacob. The Testaments were translated into Latin in the thirteenth century, but were banned from the canon three hundred years later. Genesis 25:27 paints Jacob as a simple man (*vir simplex*) living in a tent. He blessed his son, Issachar, a farmer like his father, because he too lived simply and walked in the simplicity of his eyes.[7] In the spirit of respect and generosity that animated the fifth son of Jacob, Issachar first offered his crops to the Lord, then shared his harvest with his father, keeping only what was left for himself. In recognition, the Lord doubled Issachar's harvest. Such simplicity, father and son realized, was a godsend: 'Jacob also knew that God aided my simplicity, for on every poor man and every one in distress I bestowed the good things of the earth in simplicity of heart.'[8]

Divine assistance does not dismiss Issachar's simplicity. On the contrary, the divine hand confirms the election of the simple man. In the Testament, simplicity of heart is the gift of giving. Issachar's lineage inherited his simplicity. His advice to them:

And now hearken to me, my children, and walk in simplicity of heart, for I have seen in it all that is well-pleasing to the Lord. The simple coveteth not gold, defraudeth not his neighbour, longeth not after manifold dainties, delighteth not in varied apparel, doth not picture to himself to live a long life, but only waiteth for the will of God, and the spirits of error have no power against him. For he cannot allow within his mind a thought of female beauty, that he should not pollute his mind in corruption. No envy can enter his thoughts, no jealousy melteth away his soul, nor doth he brood over gain with insatiate desire; for he walketh in uprightness of life, and beholdeth all things in simplicity, not admitting in his eyes malice from the error of the world, lest he should see the perversion of any of the commandments of the Lord.[9]

A simple heart pleases not just the one who possesses it, but also and primarily God, towards whom the heart naturally turns. The simple man obeys the commandments enumerated in the Decalogue: you shall not covet, nor by extension should you defraud others, long for what you have not, or delight in luxury. The moral imperatives that Issachar willingly obeys in all his simplicity shield him from the world of temptations.

The simple man is a fortress penetrated only by the will of God. He sees only the good in the world, not because the world is all good, but because he sees only 'in simplicity', preventing malice from entering his eyes and infesting his soul. The simple eye sees everything but admits only what pleases God, the good. The man with simple vision selects what he sees to shield from vice the faithful hand of God, who shares in all his simplicity what the earth had given him. The Testament continues:

Keep therefore the law of God, my children, and get simplicity, and walk in guilelessness, not prying over-curiously into the commands of God and the business of your neighbour; but love the Lord and your neighbour, have compassion on the poor and weak. Bow down your back unto husbandry, offering gifts unto the Lord with thanksgiving; for with the first-fruits of the earth did the Lord bless me.[10]

This passage transcribes the loving acceptance of God's commands. His mandate substitutes compassion and love for the questioning of divine orders. Admonitions listed in the Testament culminate in the glorification of agricultural labour, working the earth to offer back to God what He had offered Issachar in the first place. Simplicity is not receiving passively; simplicity is actively honouring God in all one's activities, activities governed by simple ethical principles of generosity, industriousness, assent and concern only for one's immediate entourage. The disregard of these principles, which all hail from a simple heart, leads to a crescendo of ills affecting and infecting one's lineage: 'I know, my children, that in the last times your sons will forsake simplicity, and will cleave unto avarice, and leaving guilelessness will draw near to malice, and forsaking the commandments of the Lord will cleave unto Beliar.'[11]

Although Issachar's God is merciful, the price to pay for temporarily departing from simplicity is high. The only way to stay clear of the Devil and free from the tyranny of men is to walk in simplicity. Issachar is painted as the paragon of simplicity of manners, intentions, needs, desires and faith. The lesson is that simplicity guarantees against tyranny; only when living simply will the deeds of 'malicious men' cease and the Devil flee.[12] The teleology governing Issachar's simple ethics aims at a holy reunion: 'Every wild beast shall ye subdue, having with yourselves the God of heaven walking in simplicity of heart.'[13] Simplicity will tame the wild beasts to show the grandeur of humanity marching alongside its Creator. All the exercises prompted by the simple life work towards this one end: walking in simplicity with God. Walking in simplicity means living in simplicity, the *telos* of Issacharian ethics. Aged 122, Issachar dies strong and healthy, having served his God in the simplicity of his heart. Issachar embodies the simple man and his life the simple life.

The Shepherd of Hermas, composed in the second century, was a popular Christian book of visions, mandates and parables. Hermas, a freed slave from Greece living in Rome, deems himself a simple man of modest intelligence. Once rich, he was thrown into poverty later in life. The book portrays an old woman, an allegory for the Church, who grows younger with each vision in which she appears. The shepherd, an angel of repentance, appears later in the book to deliver a series of sermon-like mandates and parables. In the second vision, Hermas learns that simplicity and guilelessness constitute the strongest defences against wickedness and vice. Although as a father he is guilty of neglecting the moral education of his children, who have fallen into apostasy, he will still be saved:

> But herein is thy salvation, in that thou didst not depart from the living God, and in thy simplicity and thy great continence. These have saved thee, if thou abidest therein; and they save all who do such things, and walk in guilelessness and simplicity. These men prevail over all wickedness, and continue unto life eternal.[14]

Simplicity, along with continence and guilelessness, protect against guile, cunning and craftiness, and open the door to eternal life. The third vision records the building of the tower upon the waters, another allegory for the Church. The tower is supported by seven women: Faith, Self-Restraint, Simplicity, Guilelessness, Chastity, Intelligence and Love. Simplicity is the allegorical daughter of Self-Restraint and the mother of Guilelessness. The shepherd who appears in the fifth vision gives Hermas twelve mandates or commandments. In the second mandate, simplicity is once again paired with guilelessness and is associated with the innocence of childhood. Simplicity and guilelessness lead the charge in an alliance against double-mindedness. For it is the divisions within the heart, the fissures in the mind or the distortions of the meanings of words that cause wretchedness and sin. Salvation requires that double-mindedness be absent from the heart and mind. Many of the mandates and parables read as exhortations to be simple-minded. The double-minded are described as neither alive nor dead in Parable Eight.[15] They cause dissensions and create divisions even among themselves. They 'have the Lord on their lips, but have Him not in their heart'.[16] Doubt and hesitations rank high in the index of sins. The double-minded man, the *dipsychos* – the two-spirited, double-souled – is easily swayed by the lies of the Beliar, the Devil.[17] This is similar to the exhortation in Wisdom of Solomon 1 cited above, where it is written that the Lord should be sought with a single, simple heart. It also occurs in the Testaments of the Twelve Patriarchs or the Twelve Sons of Jacob, as in Jeremiah 24:7: 'And I will give them an heart to know me, that I *am* the Lord: and they shall be my people, and I will be their God: for they shall return unto me with their whole heart.' The heart knows only when it is undivided, when it is simple. Only a simple heart and a simple mind may have simple and direct knowledge of a simple Being, God. For the *dipsychos*, however, there is only division and confusion. Such simplicity and unity of heart and vision can be acquired through practice, rigour and rule.

Early forms of monasticism were largely anchoritic; monks such as St Anthony of Egypt (251–356 CE) lived a solitary existence in the desert, to commune with God far from the noise and temptations of the society of men. While the lives of monks in the early Christian era were generally governed by ascetic principles, one theologian stands out for the treatment of simplicity in his works on asceticism. His name was Philoxenos. He was born in the mid-fifth century CE and was appointed Archbishop of Mabbug, in Syria, in 485. Philoxenos was a polemicist who was a staunch defender of the miaphysites, or believers in the one nature of Christ. He left a considerable body of texts in Syriac, including two discourses on simplicity. He was not a monk, but he was well acquainted with asceticism and as an archbishop he had pastoral duties towards the monks. The monasticism he promoted in his writings started with ascetic practice and culminated in divine conversation, knowledge and perfection. David Michelson writes that

> For Philoxenos, knowledge of God was attained or preserved largely through forms of praxis such as the oversight of religious communities, mystical contemplation, the reading of scripture, participation in the liturgical mysteries, and the ascetic practices of spiritual combat.[18]

His discourses are not theoretical exercises of disengagement from the world. On the contrary, they should be read as instructions for the practice of religious discipline and lectures for living a simple life, culminating in the conversation with God. The discourses follow the seven steps to perfection: faith, simplicity, fear of God, renunciation of the world, abstinence from food and drink, asceticism and sexual abstinence. For Philoxenos, simplicity defines monastic life in both its practical and its contemplative states. For him, the life of a monk should strive to replicate Edenic simplicity:

> Who does not know how much more simple was that first couple, the first ones of the human race, and how they were simple regarding the entire way of the world? They were not tempted or occupied with any of its matters, because even occupation with worldly matters had not been yet revealed. In this way they were close to [experiencing] divine visions and God was speaking face-to-face with them continuously and was found with them at all times in intimate conversation . . . He was showing them everything in detail like a human being, but they had not taken up thought about him in their mind, 'Where indeed is the dwelling of That One who was showing them? From when has he existed? If he is the one who makes, was he made? And if he is made, who is the one who made him? Why has he created us? For what reason has he placed us in this Paradise and delivered this law to us?' These things were remote from their minds because simplicity does not consider such things as these but is completely drawn to give heed to whatever it hears, and all its thought is merged entirely into the word of whoever is speaking to it, just like a child [listens] to the word of whoever is speaking with him. Look then also, God had placed simplicity in the ancient leaders of our race, and it became the recipient of the commandment.[19]

Monasticism as inspired by Adam and Eve's lives shuns judgement, questioning, doubt and speculation. In a state of Edenic simplicity, knowledge springs directly and continuously; the simple mind receives it without resistance or divided attention. It is 'drawn' to the words it hears, and its words are one with those heard. But in the postlapsarian world we inhabit, the innocent ignorance of the child provides a lesson in intellectual humility:

> I am not speaking about the [kind] of simplicity in the world that is considered to be foolishness, but the single-ness of one thought that is simple to obey and not judge, to receive and not scrutinize in the same manner that an infant also acquires words from a nurse, and even more as a youth who receives book learning from his teacher, neither judging nor scrutinizing those things that were said to him. Because just as the capacity of the infant is inadequate for the inquiry of human books, so the level of our intellect is inadequate to understand the interpretations of divine mysteries.[20]

This 'simplicity of nature' permeates all aspects of monastic life as well as the lives of solitaries in the wilderness. Simplicity means compliance to order, both monastic and divine; it is a continuous practice, first as a willed and deliberate exercise, and then progressively defining all aspects of life before ultimately becoming life itself. An important part of daily practice is to banish speculation and doubt.[21] The child in this example and in life offers a model to emulate, a point of valuable comparison ('after the manner of a child'; 'like a child'), not a state of regression. For Philoxenos, faith opens the eyes to the commandments and to simplicity understood as innocence, and it facilitates the observance of the commandments.[22] The idea dominating this passage – the exercise to engage in and the ideal to be achieved – is summed up in 'the singleness of one thought'. The multiplicity of thoughts and ideas is, as we will see, the work of the Devil. Oneness of thought is divine accord. It goes without saying that simplicity is oneness of thought, not absence of thought. Achieving simplicity of thought means achieving oneness with God, who is one and simple. The ultimate simplicity is the union of one with One, forming one.

In the second discourse on simplicity, Philoxenos posits that no one can be virtuous without first being simple. For him, simplicity is the birthplace of virtue and monasticism. In the excerpt that follows, the Archbishop of Mabbug explains that in cenobitic communities and among anchorites, simplicity renders the craftiness of the world superfluous. The passage is long, but it has the merit of drawing a clear picture of simple living as the archbishop saw it practised by monks:

Simplicity is especially appropriate for the monastic way of life, and clarity of mind greatly agrees with those who have left the world and live apart from it. Wherever there is not one of the ways of the world, the cunning of the world is also not required. We have with us here neither buying nor selling, nor is there with us any bargaining for the sake of transient profits. No one here can become greater than his brothers and be seen with more authority than his companion. No one here surpasses or is surpassed because there are no reasons for superiority among us. No fields and vineyards here are divided, neither are there lands separated by boundaries. No one here wishes to become wealthier than his brother and abound in worldly possession more than his companion. No one here wishes to be seen in resplendent clothes, for every single one of us has the humble clothing of mourning. No one here has been made a servant of his stomach and wishes to find for himself banquets of food, for we are all being fed from one common table. No one here wishes to violate the honor of his brother, for we are commanded to honor one another. No one here has gone to court against his companion, for we all take up one another's cause. No one here wishes to build nor does another desire to sketch [the plans of] palaces, because all of us have a single narrow dwelling in a cloister. No one here wishes to expand his dwelling and construct for himself gilded beds, for all of us sleep on the ground humbly in a small defined space.[23]

No commerce, no possessions, no divisions, no greed, no distrust, no grandiloquence, no superfluity. In that place there was only simplicity as the way of communal life. The eloquence of Philoxenos shines forth in this description of the simple life, where every sentence, like a refrain, commences with a simple and categorical 'No one here'. The grounded presence of the community ('here') supersedes the individual ('one') and transmutes the divisive spirit of individuality into the oneness of communal life. The community of the simples exists in a real world estranged from the world of factions and 'craftiness' and of multiplicity. 'No one here' needs to be read with the full force of the statement. The absence is in fact a full presence achieved through the exercises which determine the monk's simple life. 'No one here' renders the absolute absence of self which is yet filled with the absolute presence of God, and manifest in the simple duties rendered by all. The fulfilling presence can only be achieved through the exercise and practice of simplicity, and ultimately through simplicity as life itself.

The simple life contrasts starkly with the life of 'craftiness', deceit, cunning and multiplicity, which is the life of the many. The life of the simples replicates the life of spiritual beings: 'The entire way of life of the disciples of Jesus flourishes in simplicity. If you take simplicity away from them, you have disturbed the rule. With us simplicity is a source of pride, and whoever possesses it is wise.'[24]

Simplicity is the cornerstone of the rule: without simplicity, there is no rule; without the rule, there is no monastic life. The wise men live under the same rule in the company of wise and discerning men among whom no cunning exists. Simplicity begets clarity, as described in the previous passage, and discernment. The discerning and clear-minded simple man is called a fool in the world populated by dupes and tricksters who think of themselves as wise. In the monastery, the monk who is a fool in the world is a simple wise man, living among his fellow simples, all of them in retreat from the world.

Philoxenos believes in the simplicity, oneness and singularity of God and of disciples. True disciples are called 'simple', which is also the name of God. 'Would that you should be named by the [same] name God is called; the name of "simple" is indicative of something singular.'[25] The disciples' simplicity, however, is that of a child, who is pure, innocent and obedient. In practice, the qualities of simplicity, innocence and obedience make virtuous acts easy to carry out with diligence and promptness.[26] Although monks, like simple disciples, may not be of much use in a world of craftiness, greed and deceit, they are 'useful and necessary to the kingdom of God'.[27] Their usefulness lies in the respect they garner from other monks, inviting emulation as Christ did, by wearing simple clothing, maintaining a simple appearance and uttering simple words.[28] Just by imitating Paul or Christ, simples can withstand all the attacks and mockery levelled at them.

> In order that it will not be a burden to you to be considered by people a fool by your simplicity, God shows himself as a fool, because he was standing before his questioners without giving an answer. He was considered by them ignorant when he did not give back an answer, in order that you may also hold fast on to your soul's strength and not transgress *the law of simplicity*, not even if you are considered a fool by every person and are counted as ignorant and without education. Whoever is irritated if he is considered by someone [to be] simple and unlettered, his mind is tied to his passion of the love of the world's empty knowledge.[29]

He cared not to be seen as simple and ignorant. In following His example, disciples free themselves from the fetters of worldly knowledge and tyrannical passions. The *law of simplicity* sets them free. The shepherd and the sheep, disciples and believers 'should not depart from the law of simplicity', regardless of the ills they suffer or the false accusations they endure.[30] To craftiness, the simple combatant and disciple respond with innocence and silence. In this combat, victory is sweet: 'simplicity is without anxiety, and, on account of this, persistent joy [accompanies] it at all times.'[31]

Simplicity leaves no room for passions and cunning to agitate the soul and disturb simple joy. Like a child, the simple is permanently and peacefully joyful. We all love children and childlikeness; ergo we all love simplicity: this is the conclusion of Philoxenos.[32] That's not all: the childlikeness of the simple man wins him the trust of all men, as we tend to readily place our confidence and trust in children. In the end, even those who scorn the childlikeness of the simple ones cannot but love them.[33] Simplicity is irresistible. 'Who does not desire to be loved by God', asks Philoxenos of his listeners, 'and to be loved by people? Both of these are found in simplicity.'[34] To be loved, be simple.

Imbued with love, the simple man fears no evil, commits no evil, sees no evil, hears no evil, and says no evil. Because he is without deceit, he cannot see deceit in others.

> Simplicity believes that everyone is similar to it and thinks that [another] person considers himself just as he does, and such is the case for everyone. [Simplicity] is the mirror of its soul and the appearance of its self, and according to what is in it, so it observes in everyone else.[35]

Simplicity sees the world as it sees itself: simple, one. The transformative magic of simplicity does not elude the Syrian theologian: 'The one who is simple not only is simple but also changes whatever happens to him into this state [of simplicity].'[36] Storms are caused by the activity of opposite forces, and battles are fought between bellicose factions. In simplicity, there are no storms and no battles because true simplicity turns the many into one. Simplicity is not just a retreat from the world, or a set of rules becoming life itself; simplicity transmutes this divided world into one truer to God's Creation, singular and simple as God Himself.

After all this, Philoxenos is still faced with a dilemma: is simplicity just pure naivety and blind faith? No, because unlike true simplicity mindless naivety does not fear God. The fear of God, replicated in the fear of the child for its teacher, shows the simple to pay no heed to lies, deceit and heresy, and to dispose of worldly, bookish and speculative knowledge. Instead, the simple fears and obeys only one master and follows only one Christian path. The Incarnation occupies a central place in Philoxenian theology. The moment when the Word became flesh (John 1:14) is the moment when the distance between man and the divine was bridged. For Philoxenos, as David Michelson and André de Halleux have shown, the *becoming* man does not alter the divinity of Christ, who remains one and simple in the Incarnation. The process of *becoming* comprises the entire salvation, not just the moment of the Incarnation itself.[37] But for Philoxenos the Incarnation itself remains beyond the grasp of human understanding. Knowledge of God is not to be found in reasoning and words but through the practice of a life of simplicity, where such knowledge is received in passivity and through direct access to the divine, in a simple life that is always *becoming*.

In two other discourses, Philoxenos addresses the more practical matters of poverty, abstinence and fornication. The archbishop cautions the monks that the battle between simplicity, poverty, abstinence and the temptations of Mammon introduce duplicity of thought and allegiance. Philoxenos does not condemn riches altogether; he condemns their dominion over the rich. In the case of wealthy men like Job, riches were not an obstacle on his path to perfection because he, like Abraham, David and Isaac, remained the master of his possessions; like them, he was never possessed by his wealth.[38] In another memorable passage, Philoxenos depicts the rebirth that comes with the shedding of all possessions:

> It is said that a person takes off the world when he distances himself from everything in it and distributes his wealth and possessions completely to those who are needy. He leaves the world and departs naked alone in the same manner that he has gone out from the womb. Because in this way residence in the world is for a human being just like the natural womb is for the fetus carried in it. Just as he is still in the womb in darkness in a gloomy and damp place, not sensing any of these things of this world, and these things that are in the creation and in the place of the world outside of the womb do not ascend upon his heart, so also a person who is confined in the physical way of the world as in a womb, and his [sense of] discernment being hidden in the darkness of his worries, and his mind enshrouded in the gloom of human anxiety is not able to sense the blessings and riches in the way of Christ. Spiritual things are not apparent to him as long as his discernment is hidden in the darkness of physical things . . . Just as there [the fetus] abandons the womb and exists outside of it, so also here one should leave the world and depart from it, because the world is [configured] in the type of the womb: just as the fetus sheds the womb, a person will shed the world.[39]

To renounce material riches in order to acquire spiritual riches is a *topos* of ascetic literature. The interest of this passage lies in the metaphor of rebirth, the coming into the world followed by the progressive discovery of the real world and all its riches. This world of simplicity is not dark and damp as the womb-like world; it is lit and dry, like the desert where the monks are exhorted to live in complete poverty. After leaving the womb, senses develop, the eye finally sees, the ear hears, the tongue speaks, and so do the organs and their associated functions, as the liver for wrath and the gallbladder for enlightenment, continues Philoxenos. As senses and organs find their real and singular purpose, a simple and perfect man is *becoming*. The idea of simplicity as permanent birth will be long-lived. It will reappear in Quietism in the seventeenth century, notably in Fénelon's sermon on simplicity, and later in Rousseau's work.

The body and particularly the stomach are the objects of the following discourse, in which Philoxenos attacks greediness and enslavement by the passions, which debase man to the rank of animals, causing him to stray away from perfection in God. The second discourse shows how to exercise control over one's passions in the dark tableaux of greed and gluttony and how to free oneself from the shackles of desire. To avoid falling prey to greed and hunger one must understand their natures. Natural hunger, according to Philoxenos, occurs when the body is physically weak and no longer responsive, not just when the stomach feels empty. Understanding one's needs and desires and when to satisfy them gains one true freedom. The body becomes a site where a temporary victory over impulses can be tasted, where freedom can be experienced. But sweet as it may be, the experience of victory will dissipate if one lowers one's guard and desires regain control. For the simplification – the understanding and control – of desires and needs entails a permanent state of combat against lust, against excess, and whatever is unnecessary to life itself: 'Everything that is placed upon your dinner table and your eye sees and desires, do not think about it, but say silently to your stomach, "Because you have desired it, you will not taste it."'[40]

The exercise here is one of strengthening the will, of purification of the gaze, and of internal dialogue with one's body and desires. Philoxenos is revealing two laws that govern desires, greed and the passions: the external laws dictated by the society one lives in and internal laws, self-imposed and powerful. Knowledge gained from the observation and observance of internal laws contributes to the separation of unnatural lust from natural and simple needs. In that sense, eating simple food that you lust for is worse than eating expensive food for which you have no desire. The mechanisms of lust and desire will divulge their powerful dominion, as well as the ways to defeat them, to the simple who studies them with resolve and patience. In time, simplicity will impart the knowledge of the world: 'Climb up, therefore, and stand on the heights of knowledge and look out on the entire world from there and see its course, its lightness and its agitation, and the promise of its dwellers on all sides.'[41] From lust spring excess, theft, commerce, industry, slavery and war. And all these ills are imputable to the 'lust of the belly'.[42] For this reason, the body should remain under the strict control of the simple soul:

> Just as the eye receives through its rapid [movements] the vision of the simplicity of light, so also the soul's vision receives the clarity and simplicity of spiritual knowledge after the victory over these physical passions. Just as the ordinary sun falling on natures and various bodies seems to them to be cut and divided, while its single nature is

simple in which there is no division, in the same way also is spiritual knowledge when it has risen on the ways of life and labors: it seems to them that it is separated and divided, while with its soul it is a unique and simple [knowledge]. The soul is not worthy to receive the rising of this light, unless one has first been born from the physical nature to the spiritual nature, [one's] birth being completed through labors and austerities.[43]

Labours and austerities governed by the law of monastic simplicity transmute carnality into spirituality and change division into oneness. The constant practice of simplicity in discreet exercises and practices brings forth the knowledge of simplicity as oneness. Simple acts *become* simplicity. This constant *becoming* of simplicity in simple labours and austerities would determine the lives of many monks. Giorgio Agamben's study of monastic life aids in the understanding of the nature of such lives. Monastic life, a life where the rule or 'law of simplicity' should not be disturbed according to Philoxenos, is a life where simplicity is a form of life. To quote Agamben, it is a 'form-of-life, that is to say, a life that is linked so closely to its form that it proves to be inseparable from it'.[44] Here, simplicity as form and simplicity as life *become* one and indivisible.

The vocation to join a cenobitic order, to live a life of simplicity among a community of like-minded simple men or women, often originates in an epiphany, a moment when the hustle and bustle of the world disappears all at once, when the complexity of existence is condensed into a simple and irrevocable truth. 'The greatest religions are all, in fact, very simple,' wrote Thomas Merton, who suggested that:

They all retain very important essential differences, no doubt, but in their inner reality Christianity, Buddhism, Islam and Judaism are extremely simple (though capable as I say of baffling luxuriance) and they all end up with the simplest and most baffling thing of all: direct confrontation with Absolute Being, Absolute Love, Absolute Mercy or Absolute Void, by an immediate and fully awakened engagement in the living of everyday life.[45]

Merton asserted that one can only understand a religion, in this case Buddhism, when one meets it in an 'existential manner, in a person in whom it is alive'.[46] The simple life of the monk enables the experience of the Absolute: in the simple life, little, if anything, hinders the emergence of the Absolute in the living, in the present, because the consciousness of the monk is awakened to all possibilities, including the possibility of encountering the Absolute in the string of minute tasks that constitute a devout life. In the living of simplicity, all, the Absolute, can happen. For Merton, simplicity starts in the 'engagement in the living of everyday life' and culminates in the spiritual union with God.

Thomas Merton was a Trappist monk in the Abbey of Gethsemani, Kentucky. Trappists or members of the Order of Cistercian of the Strict Observance (OCSO) follow closely the Rule of Saint Benedict, laid down in the sixth century. The Rule is governed by three main principles: poverty, chastity and obedience. The Trappist movement originated in the seventeenth century, when Armand-Jean le Bouthillier de Rancé, the abbot at La Trappe, France, instituted an austere regime to counter the decline in devout practice in Cistercian monasteries. Men and women of few words, but not committed to silence, Trappists and

Trappistines lived and still live simple communal lives dominated by prayer and work. Except for the sick, members of the OCSO who are in good health refrain from eating the meat of four-legged animals as prescribed in the Rule of Saint Benedict. Their lives are lived in the quasi-permanent company of brethren and sisters.

In the twentieth century, two Trappist monks gained fame outside of the order, one for his participation in social reforms, Thomas Merton, the other, Thomas Keating, for his leading role in the creation of Contemplative Outreach. Through Centring Prayer, Contemplative Outreach aims to reinvigorate the contemplation tradition and contemplative practice in Christianity. Contemplative prayer has a long and rich tradition in Christianity, from the Desert Fathers to the medieval mystics to the spiritual writers of the seventeenth century. It is often described as a surrender to God's presence or as a divine union sought by God and welcomed by the believer without effort, whether intellectual or imaginative. Contemplative prayer can take several forms, but one common method is the recitation of a single word or simple phrase excerpted from the Scriptures, or simply the name of Jesus. It has been referred to as the Prayer of Simplicity and Prayer of Simple Regard.

Centring Prayer has a seven-stage structure that gradually leads the self to surrender to God's presence and the divine manifestations within it. The seven stages are silence, solitude, solidarity, service, stillness, simplicity and, finally, surrender. Simplicity is

> the integration of contemplation and action, a growing capacity to live in the midst of duality – the ups and downs of daily life – without losing the non-dual perspective.

Contemplation is not the same as action. They are distinct but they are not separate.[47]

Simplicity happens after stillness or the experience of God's presence in oneself and before surrender, a moment of unity with God, and eternal life. In Centring Prayer, simplicity can be described as a union when two become one while remaining two, distinct but not separate. Importantly, in the stage of simplicity one acquires the ability to live simply, or non-dually, in a complex world rife with tension and oppositions. Thomas Keating has also defined simplicity as 'the integration and unification of human capacities'; for him simplicity is the interconnectedness of all components of the world, each acting in accord with its own capacities and 'integrated into the more developed level of consciousness'.[48] This level of consciousness opens on to the divine will.[49] More practically, simplicity is achieved through 'simplicity of life style and a life of prayer'.[50] The simple life is one that maintains the unity of the self in the face of divisive actions, thoughts and emotions. For Keating, 'simplicity is the union of contemplation and action in our daily lives.'[51] In the simple life one is present to one's action and contemplation, a life where contemplation and action are united, where one does not happen without the other, where action is contemplation and contemplation action. That is simple living.

Thomas Merton was a prolific writer and possibly one of the best-known American theologians of the twentieth century. He spoke out many times in favour of interfaith dialogues, peace and social justice. He entered the monastery at the Abbey of Gethsemani in December 1941. Four years later the Abbot of Gethsemani, Dom Frederic Dunne, asked him to translate a short text written in French by a Trappist monk, Dom Jean-Baptiste Chautard, and published in 1928. Merton took to the task and wrote what is known as *The Spirit of Simplicity*, comprising a translation of the French text followed by Merton's own commentaries on St Bernard of Clairvaux's views on interior simplicity. The commentaries open with a reminder that simplicity is the cornerstone of Cistercian spirituality. The first step towards a simple life consists of recognizing one's duplicity. Duplicity can then be overcome by the practice of simplicity understood as humility or self-effacement. Merton describes simplicity as three mortifications: the 'uncompromising mortification of lower appetites' such as hunger, clothing and lifestyle; then the mortification of the 'interior senses and the intellect', which translates as simplicity in devotion and studies; and finally the mortification of the will, the most important of the three.[52] The virtue of obedience or simplification of the will is one of the greatest virtues. Simplicity of obedience is not blind subordination to power; it is obedience directed by three principles or *nihils*. *Nihil plus* (nothing more): the will adds nothing to what is asked of it, in other words it resists the temptation of zealousness and it does not seek the grandeur found in sacrifice; *nihil minus* (nothing less): self-will does less than is demanded of it to satisfy a self-interest or self-love; and finally *nihil aliter* (nothing other): the will changes nothing in what is asked of us whether it is asked by a brother, a superior or God. Adding nothing to the rule, substracting nothing from it, changing nothing in it help simplify the will and prepare it for willing obedience.[53]

For Merton, writing after St Bernard, the simplification of the will entails not simply a surrender to the will of God but submission to the *voluntas communis*, the common will. The common will acting for the common good emanates from God and is relayed via the superiors and brethren.[54] Self-will and selfsatisfaction block the expression of the common will, and in the worst cases pervert it. Unhappiness, for instance, results from the tensions between the three wills: self-will, the will of others and the will of God. Peace and love spring from the simplicity or union of all wills. '*Lack of peace is identified with a certain lack of simplicity, a lack of union, harmony with circumstances and events.* Simplicity thus takes on the sense of *abandonment*,' writes Merton.[55] The abandonment, he adds, is not a passive surrendering as found in Quietism but rather an '*active desire that God's will be done*'.[56] A simple life is a life spent willing the simplicity or union of all wills, willing that God's will imbues the common will. A will that wills is a more perfect simplicity, in the words of the Trappist and his saint. The greatest simplicity occurs in the mystical union with God in infused contemplation. Suffice it to say that the union with God is spiritual, not substantial, as we could not become one substance with God.[57] However: 'the union of *wills*, making us one spirit with God, is the highest and purest and most intimate union that can possibly be achieved by two individuals remaining essentially distinct. This is the culminating ideal of Cistercian simplicity!'[58]

In this union, the ideal of simplicity for the Trappist, the soul finally becomes itself as it loses itself in God. Merton had presented the idea of the likeness of the soul to God in his introduction. In his final chapter, in the ideal of simplicity as he sees it, he posits that the soul unified with God becomes itself because it is like God. Having lost its will and interests, the unified soul attains 'this supereminent perfection of simplicity' where it '*loves itself exactly as God loves it*'.[59] In the most perfect simplicity self-love is but love of God. This beatification of the soul is the result of a life lived in obedience, humility, charity and simplicity. In the words of Merton:

> The culmination of Cistercian simplicity is the mystical marriage of the soul with God, which is nothing else but the perfect union of our will with God's will, made possible by the complete purification of all the duplicity of error and sin. This purification is the work of love and particularly of the love of God in our neighbor. Hence it is inseparable from that social simplicity which consists in living out the *voluntas communis* in actual practice. This is the reason for the Cistercian insistence on the common life: the Cistercian is almost never physically alone. He has opportunities to give up his will to others twenty-four hours a day. It is precisely this which, according to the mind of St Bernard, St Aelred, and our other fathers, *should prepare him most rapidly for the mystical marriage.*[60]

Simplicity is union, a union with fellow men as preparation for the perfect union with God.

In his final years, Thomas Merton sought solitude in Gethsemani, but most of his life was spent in the company of others, preparing in simplicity for the ultimate simplicity of life in contemplative union with God. In his conversion experience, social activism and extensive knowledge of the world and of theology, he was the equal of another polymath whose influence, spirituality and radical views profoundly affected twentieth-century activist and anarchist circles. Jacques Ellul was Professor of History, Sociology and Political Studies at the University of

Bordeaux, France. He is best known for *The Technological Society*, just one among some fifty of his works on theology, sociology and technology. First published in French in 1954 and translated into English ten years later, *The Technological Society* sparked Merton's interest. He praised the book and took extensive notes while reading it.[61] His views, however, changed as he continued his reading of Ellul's work. He found him too pessimistic and thought his analysis to be weak at times. Merton gave hope a greater place in his worldview than Ellul ever did, while the latter saw his fellow men as relinquishing their very humanity to technology. But as Gordon Oyer has shown, Merton had only limited access to Ellul's oeuvre and probably failed to appreciate that the Frenchman's display of extreme pessimism was a rhetorical tool to open people's eyes to the menace of technology. Merton was largely unacquainted with Ellul's theological works – notably, his concept of Christian hope. Hope is what is left to humans in a technological world abandoned by God, according to Ellul. For the Christian and anti-technology militant he was, hope took the form of 'active waiting', as waiting is of no use to technological cultures avid for immediate action and efficiency. Second, hope was to be found in prayer that seeks to enter, hopefully, into a dialogue with God. And, finally, he viewed hopeful pessimism as a way of deconstructing power structures. Hope, Ellul believed, tests passive subservience and powerlessness to the point of action, and political action in some cases.[62] Writing at a time of accelerated technological progress, both Merton and Ellul appreciated the perils of blind hopelessness and the necessity of action.

In addition, Merton was taken with Hannah Arendt's work, *The Human Condition*. In his reading notes, he wrote:

1. *Vita Activa* [the active life] lost its point of reference in contemplation – thereby becoming purely active – i.e., degenerating from *political action* to *fabrication* to *laboring* and finally to that completely empty activity of *job holding.*
2. Being has been replaced by *process.* The process is everything. Mod[ern] man sees only how to fit without friction into productive process and in this he finds 'happiness'.[63]

In a life lived in simplicity, action is not segregated from contemplation. It is in partaking of and acting with the common will that man first experiences communion with others as a preliminary to the contemplative union with God. The ultimate spiritual marriage is actively willed, as Merton has shown, from a will that is progressively more selfless to become ultimately God's. Action without contemplation is dominated by self-will and paradoxically and dangerously guided by blindness: in contemplation, on the other hand, one can see with the gaze of God. Pure action is blind and blinding. The degeneration from political action to job holding that Merton has identified in his notes is one of disengagement with others and the world. In the end, the self is holding itself together by the thread of an idea, that of a job. So we witness action turning into an 'empty activity', having 'lost its point of reference in contemplation'.

In the second note, Merton addresses another of his main concerns, which is also related to simplicity. The 'fitting without friction' is that which makes the union between two possible. Here, simplicity as the path of least resistance is perverted and no longer serves the greatest happiness found in the love of and by God. Derailed as it is in a world of empty activity, simplicity breeds alienation from others and servitude to technology and power. But for Merton, true simplicity is mercy, the mercy we receive from God and share with our neighbour. Simplicity is unity of self among others. Above his notes on Arendt, Merton commented on some poems he had just read. He preferred the simpler ones: 'the religious ones are often the most simple and direct of all. Simplicity = Sacredness. These poems prove the essential and deep connection.'[64] Simplicity is sacredness when it connects without friction, not when it alienates without friction.

So Merton, for his part, was taken by Ellul's idea of the perils of technology. But technology for Ellul is just a subset of something greater and more menacing:

> The term *technique*, as I use it, does not mean machines, technology, or this or that procedure for attaining an end. In our technological society, *technique* is the *totality of methods rationally arrived at and having absolute efficiency* (for a given stage of development) in *every* field of human activity.[65]

Whereas Merton saw the perilous vacuity of activity, Ellul believed the saturation of human activity with the idea of efficiency to have advanced to the extent that the words 'activity' and 'efficiency' have become interchangeable. And whereas Merton, with Arendt, saw Process as replacing Being, Ellul sees technique and efficiency vampirizing Being:

> Technique has penetrated the deepest recesses of the human being. The machine tends not only to create a new human environment, but also to modify man's very

essence. The milieu in which he lives is no longer his. He must adapt himself, as though the world were new, to a universe for which he was not created. He was made to go six kilometers an hour, and he goes a thousand. He was made to eat when he was hungry and to sleep when he was sleepy; instead, he obeys a clock. He was made to have contact with living things, and he lives in a world of stone. He was created with a certain essential unity, and he is fragmented by all the forces of the modern world.[66]

Ellul and Merton witnessed the creation of new beings engineered by a force gone out of human control. In this new world, God is robbed of his Creation and man is robbed of his existential unity. Efficiency and process do not produce the mere modification of being; they are the end of being. The death of being precipitates the end of the manifestation of the common will and in the end of simplicity in God.

Technique is remarkably absent from Ellul's prelapsarian Eden. Eden is the work of God. As such it is complete and does not need any modifications, *nihil plus, nihil minus, nihil aliter*. Here is Ellul's commentary on Genesis 1:

Within creation there was work without necessity (Adam would not die of hunger if he stopped working), work without finality, without production. It was not work to gather a surplus, to make a living, to produce: it was work for *nothing*. The fruits and the produce, that which was necessary for Adam's life, all were freely given by God – not in exchange for work, a duty, an obligation, but truly gratuitously – without a connection between necessity and work. There was no causal link between work and the produce which was solely within the order of creation. Work was not useful, but free.[67]

We can see that technique is not a part of this world where work is free and willed. Technique is a product of the Fall. After the Fall man needs to work for his subsistence; work becomes an existential necessity, 'a product of necessity and not of human freedom', writes Ellul at the conclusion of his essay.[68] For Ellul, who rejected the word 'Fall', preferring 'rupture' instead, Eden and the world we live in today are diametrically opposed. Here is how he sees the world before the rupture, before technique:

> Everything was truly a whole and the plenitude of God filled everything... What end was there to pursue in these conditions, and by what means? What possible meaning could there be to the notion of means, when everything was given within the unity of being ... The whole was entrusted to Adam to manage, but there were no particulars that Adam could appropriate to himself. Only when the unity of creation was shattered did things separate, with each element taking on a particular destiny, so that there is a relationship of man to individual things. Only then, when a particular relationship had been established, could anything be called property. If we understand this miraculous universality, then to the same extent can we understand that there could not have been technique – no genus or species of technique – because technique is never anything but a collection of means and the search for the most efficient means. These two elements were radically excluded.[69]

There was no private property and no technique because there were no means: here is the picture of Eden – whole, with nothing to add. In this world, communications between man and God are direct and immediate; no technique is necessary because 'there was no force to exert.'[70] Eden is frictionless, everything gives and is given. In Eden, concludes Ellul, the idea of 'more' would have been foreign.[71] The world of 'more', of technique and efficiency, is the world of the fallen, our world. To live simply then requires that one no longer thinks of means, efficiency and property; to lead a simple life is to wait, not passively, but actively, in communion, and to live in community with others and with God under the law of simplicity.

THREE

THE 'GIFT TO BE SIMPLE'

On 19 May 1774 Ann Lee boarded a ship headed for America. With her were eight men and women searching for a simple life where all would be equal, where hands would be put to work and hearts given to God. In her native Manchester she had suffered persecution for her faith. In Colonial America, she would be persecuted for her convictions, but with perseverance and charisma, she would create an enduring utopian society that was to emblematize simplicity for generations to come – the United Society of Believers in Christ's Second Appearing, also known as the Shakers. Central to the Shakers' faith and way of life is simplicity. Their song 'Simple Gifts', memorialized by Aaron Copland, weaves together the main themes of simple living that still dictate the lives of the two remaining Shakers today:

> 'Tis the gift to be simple, 'tis the gift to be free,
> 'Tis the gift to come down where we ought to be,
> And when we find ourselves in the place just right,
> 'Twill be in the valley of love and delight.
> When true simplicity is gain'd
> To bow and to bend we shan't be asham'd

To turn, to turn will be our delight
'Till by turning, turning, we come 'round right.[1]

Composed in 1848, some sixty years after Ann Lee's death, by Elder Joseph Brackett of the Alfred Shaker Village in Maine, 'Simple Gifts' has become a staple of American folk music. The simple lyrics and melody of the song evoke the simple lives of early Americans and conjures the idea of a past long gone when everything was presumably less demanding and complicated. 'Simple Gifts' was conceived as a quick dance. The line 'to turn, to turn will be our delight' needs to be taken literally. It is the cue for the dancers to change directions in what would have been a ring dance performed by the assembly of Believers on worship days. In this song, as in many of the 10,000 spirituals composed by the Shakers, the lyrics have a quality that is more than just edifying, symbolic or even poetic – their simple words are performative. Words are realized in the actions they motivate just as they evaporate into them. In the plain liturgical economy of the single-verse song and the accompanying quick dance, words and actions can become one because they are simple in form and content. Here, the word *is not* in excess of action, it *is* action, much like action *is* the word in a simple symbiotic relationship called simplicity.

Neither austere nor exuberant, 'Simple Gifts' captures the energy of Shaker lives. The song celebrates three gifts and fundamentals of the Shaker faith: the gifts to be simple, to be free and to 'come down where one ought to be'. As 'gifts', simplicity, freedom and belonging are manifestations of extraordinary origins, be they God, Mother Ann herself or a departed one. The individual 'instrument' who receives the gift, in song, dance or in any other activities, is not the final destination of that which is being gifted. Although they may take the form of a singular manifestation investing one person, spiritual gifts are meant to be shared among members of the community. Another song, 'Balls of Simplicity', illustrates this point:

My brethren and Sisters
I've got some little balls of Simplicity.
My blessed Father James did give them unto me,
O will you have some, they will make you free.[2]

It is common in Shaker songs for concepts such as simplicity to assume a physical form, here the 'balls of Simplicity', as if to weigh down the loftiness of a concept, to reify it and submit it to the laws of earthly gravity. As in the case of performative language, metaphors have the effect of grounding, evoking the descent of gifts from the spiritual to the material. In this song, the balls of simplicity gifted by the departed Father James to the anonymous instrument have the ability to free the receiver, as well as the singers and dancers. As in 'Simple Gifts', freedom proceeds from simplicity.

Gifts are by nature transient; they manifest in word-actions and are then passed on, received by others and transmitted again. Gifted simplicity continually instigates and sustains interpersonal relations while uniting all members of the community in obligation to a liberating mutualism. For the Shakers, simplicity is a gift that keeps on giving in an unending chain of willed reciprocities and mutuality. The unifying, self-propagating and contagious quality of simplicity makes one and all free and equal. A 'bowing song' puts into music, words and steps the idea that when simplicity, freedom and humility dance to the same tune a better society is born, even if that means first stumbling on a simple little stone:

I will bow and be simple,
I will bow and be free,
I will bow and be humble,
Yea bow like the willow tree.
I will bow this is the token,
I will wear the easy yoke,
I will bow and be broken,
Yea I'll fall upon the rock.[3]

This is a beautifully simple song where the three concepts of simplicity, freedom and humility materialize into a lithe yet robust tree, a metaphor recalling Pascal's 'thinking reed'. But unlike the Pascalian reed, which stands for self-knowledge and ultimately human superiority over all of Creation, the Shaker is willingly broken upon the rock. The simplicity of the form, words and rhythm, which facilitate the transmission of the song, somehow masks the complexity of the message. With a reference to Matthew 21:41–4 in the last line, the gifted song quoted above reminds the singers and dancers that a simple stone, Christ, once rejected as the lowly son of a carpenter, became the cornerstone of a spiritual edifice. 'Whoever falls on this stone will be broken,' says the parable, but it also says that they will be pieced back together if they believe that a simple man can heal them. A different fate awaits whomever that stone shall fall upon, as they will be crushed into dust with no possibility of being one again.

Not all gifts manifested themselves in joyful songs and dances. During a particularly exalted worship service, Shakers in Union Village, Ohio, were guided 'to stoop down and eat simplicity off of the floor'.[4] Although the act of eating simplicity off the floor may evoke the call for humility in 'Simple Gifts' and the reification of simplicity in 'I Will Bow', the message of this particular manifestation is rather enigmatic. Ecstatic manifestations with equivocal messages and theatrical physicality such as this one became more common as the sect grew. At the height of Shakerism in the mid-nineteenth century, worship services became increasingly punctuated by songs and dances of divine inspiration; yet the messages of such enthused manifestations or gifts did not necessarily lend themselves well to straightforward interpretations and communal applicability. During such times of religious enthusiasm, known as the Era of Manifestations, Shakerism expanded westward and attracted throngs of new and younger recruits. The excess of some of the exalted manifestations, especially among younger converts, raised suspicions about the veracity of the gifts themselves and the truthfulness of the messengers. Such manifestations created a spiritual and social rift between the 'instruments' of the gifts, some of them charismatic leaders who could move believers through songs, dances and speeches, and those among the more traditional members of the communities who preferred ministerial and communal humility, simplicity and order.[5]

With the 1840s came the ordering of the Society and the establishment of codes of conduct published as the *Millennial Laws* of 1845, a stricter version of the 1821 laws. By the end of the Era of Manifestations in the 1860s, Shaker laws had become more restrictive, dictating lives and daily activities down to the colour of a Believer's bedsheets. These laws also reinforced aspects of Shakerism that estranged the communities from the world of unbridled greed surrounding them while safeguarding their fundamental beliefs in economic, social, sexual and racial equality. Although they were relaxed in later editions, the *Millennial Laws* continued to reinforce the three pillars of Shaker faith and communal life – utility, honesty and simplicity.

The *Summary View of the Millennial Church* enunciates twelve primary Christian virtues, the sixth of which is simplicity:

> True gospel simplicity implies a godly sincerity, and a real *singleness* of heart, in all conversation and conduct. This virtue is the operation of holiness and goodness, and produces in the soul a perfect *oneness* of character, in all things; its thoughts, words and works are plain and simple ... It is harmless and undefiled, and wholly *unmixed* with any evil. It is without ostentation, parade and any vain show, and naturally leads to plainness in all things. In all the objects of its pursuits, in all the exercise of its powers, in all its communications of good to others, it is governed solely by the will of God, and shows forth its peculiar *singleness* of heart and mind in all things.[6]

Simplicity, according to the *Summary*, is the virtue of oneness of character, actions, thoughts and words. As a primary virtue, it is everlasting and it cannot be modified.[7] Seven moral principles extracted from the twelve virtues govern the lives of the Believers. The fifth principle, 'simplicity of language', is the operation of the virtue of simplicity. It follows that words need not be many and that they may only convey the truth, that all honorific titles should be banned from the Society, and that even the 'vain addresses of *Sir* and *Madam*, *Mister* and *Miss*' may not be used among Believers.[8] Simplicity, or the virtue of oneness, dictates that the community of Believers may not be splintered by divisive hierarchies. Following the simplicity of the Gospel, all members are brethren and sisters in the oneness of the Society and the communications between them are simple in expression and truthful in content. The honesty of heart and simplicity of language ensure the 'proper respect towards our fellow men; and safely conduct us through all the scenes in this mortal life'.[9]

In the early nineteenth century, under the influence of two leaders, Joseph Meacham and Lucy Wright, Shakerism opted for the form of communalism for which it is known today. Shakers consecrate all their properties, labour and the fruit of their labour to their community; they are celibate, pacifist and egalitarian. They live apart from the world but have had an impact on American culture that is profound. Although separated from the world, they accepted 'non-communal' members who did not have to renounce marriage and who could live outside of the Shaker villages. 'Winter Shakers', those destitute men and women who converted in the autumn and left in the spring, were never turned away when they arrived in Shaker communities in November. To their immediate neighbours, or the 'World's people', Shakers sold herbal remedies, produce and furniture. As early as the late eighteenth century, Shakers started to sell seeds. This initiative turned into a lucrative mail-order business in the following century. On the sales lists were simples, or medicinal plants, of course. Shakers are credited with being the first to package seeds into small labelled paper pockets that could be posted. Shaker peddlers travelled the northeastern states selling seeds and Shaker inventions.[10] Shakers did not reject progress. With inventions ranging from the flat broom, the clothes peg and the circular saw to the wheel-driven washing machine, they contributed to a series of household innovations that has come to define a modern lifestyle.

But it is for the simplicity of their furniture that they remain best known today. From the Shakers we have retained objects with simple lines and unequivocal utility. For the many unsung artisans in the Society, the simplicity of the processes and the means of production they employed and constantly perfected were as significant as the simplicity of the objects they produced. Simplicity for them was both a means and an end. Shakers believed in perfectibility and progress so long as it was useful for the greater good of the community. They considered their daily activities to be occasions for actuating the human perfectibility gifted to them by God. Sweeping the floor, turning wood or packing seeds were meaningful and mindful activities in which the individual communed with God. The industriousness and creativity of the Shakers were expressions of something both greater than them and manifest in them. 'Shakerism', wrote Brother Theodore Johnson in the *Shaker Quarterly*, 'values human fulfilment highly and believes that man fulfils himself by being nothing more nor less than himself.'[11] Being oneself, nothing more or nothing less, means being simple. Simplicity as self-fulfilment is both the right and the responsibility of the Believer. As a right, simplicity grants one the individual freedom to be fully oneself and self-fulfil; as a responsibility, simplicity dictates the rules for communal living, industry and good economy.

In the 1920s, as Shaker communities were dwindling, collectors started to show interest in their furniture. Two such collectors were Edward Deming Andrews and Faith Andrews. They recalled their first experience in 1923 in Hancock Shaker Village, where they had stopped to buy bread:

A soft-voiced Shaker sister welcomed us warmly. We bought two loaves of bread. And in the long clean 'cookroom' we saw much besides: a trestle table, benches, rocking chairs, built-in cupboards, cooking arches, all beautiful in their simplicity. Later, eating the bread, we knew that our appetite would not be satisfied with the bread alone.[12]

The couple amassed one of the finest collections of Shaker furniture and wrote extensively on the sect. But at the time of their first visit, they did not know that the Shakers had been selling their furniture through mail-order catalogues and showrooms since the mid-nineteenth century. They could not predict that some pieces were about to cross the Atlantic and have a long-lasting impact on furniture design. What they perceived and appreciated, though, was the beautiful simplicity of Shaker forms. In 1927 Kaare Klint, architect, furniture designer and co-director of the Museum of Decorative Arts in Copenhagen, received an armed ladder-back Shaker rocking chair. Klint, who started the modern Danish furniture design movement, known for its minimalism and functionalism, was immediately taken with the simple lines of the chair. Not long after, the Museum exhibited one of these chairs. The inspirational pieces were identified as Shaker only after the publication of the Andrews' book *Shaker Furniture* in 1937. Two years later, Børge Mogensen of the Danish Cooperative Wholesale Society spearheaded the mass production of simple-lined furniture, also inspired by Shaker designs. The mass production and exportation of Shaker-inspired furniture, chairs, tables and cabinets flooded the European and American markets. With the growing fashion for Shaker-style furniture came the commodification of their faith and culture. By the 1960s, 'Shaker' meant good-quality products with simple lines. The change in the way Shakers were perceived prompted Sister R. Mildred Barker to say: 'I would like to be remembered as one who had pledged myself to the service of God and had fulfilled that pledge as perfectly as I can – not as a piece of furniture.'[13]

Shaker-inspired style with its clean lines and functionality dominated both sides of the Atlantic in the 1960s, when Shaker simplicity entered mainstream culture and many households. At the same time, not surprisingly perhaps, Shaker and Japanese designs cross-fertilized, especially in the works of American-born George Nakashima, the self-proclaimed 'Japanese Shaker'. In his study of Shaker furniture, Christian Becksvoort has shown that, as in Japanese designs, Shaker furniture never stifled the natural expressiveness of the wood, while still exposing joints in solid wood constructions.[14] The unobstructed exposure of what 'speaks', the grain of the wood, and what 'connects', the joints, emblematize Shaker design with its openness, unmediated utility and humility. The famous Shaker oval box, however beautiful we may find it, is just that, a box with a distinct vocation, to contain; and it should be seen as a box even when it appears behind glass in one of the most famous museums in the world. From July 2016 to August 2017, the Metropolitan Museum of Art in New York City hosted an exhibition of Shaker furniture and textiles showcasing how Shaker designs intersect with other traditions and art forms.[15]

The artists in the design collective Furnishing Utopia continue to pay homage to the endurance of Shaker simplicity with a series of exhibitions of Shaker-inspired furniture in Stockholm, New York and the Shaker Hancock Village.[16] Such designers perpetuate the Shakers' way that 'all beauty that has no foundation in use, soon grows distasteful and needs continuous replacement with something new.'[17] These beautiful objects, which fetch exorbitant prices today, had a different value for their makers. While we admire the craftsmanship and minimalism of Shaker artefacts, most of them museum pieces, Shakers were keen on recycling any piece that had outlived its immediate function. Their simple objects were part of a dynamic economy of transformation and optimization of material. Not only could objects be recycled, their unassuming, simple lines allowed them to easily meld with their environments – unlike more stylized pieces, whose beauty lies in their ostentatious distinctiveness and separateness. Like a Shaker, a Shaker object should not be judged to be more than it is. 'To be truly simple is to know one's self honestly, yielding neither to pride nor to false humility.'[18] What is true of the makers, is true of their creations.

Shakerism is the epitome of simplicity. We remember the excellence of Shaker craftsmanship and design, but we forget that their god was both male and female, that they welcomed all races into their villages, that their simplicity is not one of appearance or surface but of profundity: a deep simplicity. Their hope was to create a heaven on earth. But their dedication to celibacy and pacifism, as well as external factors like unchecked consumerism, hindered the expansion of Shakerism. Internal disputes also contributed to tensions, divisions and the closing of communities. Today, Shakers are part and parcel of Americana and American primitivism. Their objects and their two remaining members are intrusions of the past into the present. 'Can we still welcome them?' is a question posed by Tim Clark in a straightforward article published in 1980 about his experience among Shakers:

And the making of the Shakers into Americana is a violation of that Shaker virtue we claim to cherish most – simplicity.

But somehow I am confident that a faith that survived mob violence in the past . . . will survive the corrupting affections of this carnal world. I can say that because I have seen Shaker simplicity triumph even in the midst of one of the most carnal places on earth – New York City . . .

I saw it again on a Sunday morning in the soaring neo-Gothic vastness of Manhattan's Trinity Church, where a small party of Shakers and their worldly friends gathered for a service – a Shaker service, in a setting so riotously unsimple that the enterprise seemed doomed from the start.

But we got up in turn, and spoke, and prayed. We sang together . . .

'Tis the gift to be simple . . . [etc.]

I watched, and listened, and struggled with my own self-consciousness, which is the great enemy of simplicity.[19]

Tim Clark is not a Shaker but like them he understood that simplicity is the muting of an imperious self-consciousness that is ultimately disillusioned about itself. 'Be what you seem to be, and seem to be what you really are, and don't carry two faces under one hood,' said Father James Whittaker, one of the eight recluses who crossed the Atlantic with Ann Lee in 1774. This self-understanding, hailing partly from voluntary confessions, is called simplicity.[20]

At noon on 20 January 2009, Yo-Yo Ma, Itzhak Perlman, Anthony McGill and Gabriela Montero played a classical quartet composed by John Williams. At noon that day, Barack Obama became the 44th president of the United States of America. The title of the piece composed for the inauguration is 'Air and Simple Gifts'. The Shaker hymn is woven into a complex musical fabric, within which it struggles to convey ideas of austerity, patriotism, solemnity, profundity and 'clean, honest, all-American values', according to the *Washington Post*.[21] Because of weather conditions detrimental to musical instruments that day, the piece was pre-recorded, played and mimed on Inauguration Day. On several occasions, the new president turned towards the silent instruments pretending to be moved by the solemn music, all this in a great game of political make-believe. Not much was left of Shaker simplicity that day. It was no different on 20 January 1993, when Marilyn Horne with all her mezzo-soprano virtuosity sang 'Simple Gifts' for the inauguration of Bill Clinton. In 1985, on 20 January, the Wagnerian Jessye Norman sang the Shaker song for the newly elected Ronald Reagan. On these days, a simple song dressed up for the occasion was there to remind world leaders to remain simple. Lesson learnt?

Shakerism started with the Wardley Society in Bolton, north of Manchester, in the eighteenth century before it was developed and exported by Ann Lee to the New World. James and Jane Wardley were originally Quakers who had parted with the Society of Friends in 1747. Although both groups shared some religious and social values, Shakers trace their origins to a group of French Huguenots who came to England in the early eighteenth century. The French Prophets, as they were called, were Protestants who had fled from persecution in their native Cévennes in the south of France. They arrived in England in 1706. 'In the beginning of the eighteenth century, Spiritualism broke out on the continent of Europe, and was followed by the most remarkable religious revivals; out of which arose the "French prophets", wrote Frederick William Evans, a Shaker historian. He continued:

> These were wrought upon in a very extraordinary manner; not only in their minds, but also in their physical systems. They had visions and trances, and were subject to violent agitations of the body. Men and women, and even little children were struck with great wonder and astonishment... They continued their prophetic warnings (under much persecution) for several years, over the greater part of Europe. And, in the year 1706, the revival extended to England, where it spread far and wide. About the year 1747, some members of the Society of Quakers, who had become subjects of the revival, formed themselves into a society, of which Jane and James Wardley were the lead. Of this little society Ann Lee and her parents were members.[22]

Like the Shakers to whom they were to give rise, the French Prophets were expatriates whose convictions seemed to grow with their peregrinations. They were millennialists and spiritualists, and their enthused religiosity manifested itself in an ecstatic fervour recalling the religious enthusiasm of early Quakers in mid-seventeenth-century England. Their influence was diffuse, but traces of their beliefs can be found in Shakerism and Rousseau's natural religion. One of the symbolic daughters of the French Prophets was Marie Huber, born in 1695 in Geneva, the birthplace of Rousseau. Marie Huber's works were translated into German and English. In her 1736 book *The World Unmask'd; or, The Philosopher the Greatest Cheat*, a fictitious dialogue between three philosophers, Marie Huber presents the holy trinity of simplicity, unity and universalism:

> If Universality and Unity are inseparable, Simplicity is not less so from both. What is simple must be universal; otherwise it wou'd not be simple. What is not composed of several Parts is one: what is one, is simple. We have demonstrated that what is one is universal. *Ergo*, what is simple is universal, and one; as what is one, is simple and universal.[23]

For the Pietist and Rationalist Marie Huber, universalism is indistinguishable from simplicity and unity. Divine simplicity means that God cannot be divided into parts and that God is identical to His attributes. For example, God does not have goodness as an attribute; God *is* goodness. Universalists such as Huber believe that this world is a passing phase in God's infinite goodness and that ultimately all men and women of all the ages will return to the original goodness and oneness in a universal reconciliation. This branch of universalism negates the possibility of eternal damnation and professes salvation for all. Here, simplicity is more than a code of conduct or ideal to achieve. It is a fundamental principle on which rest an entire worldview and eschatology. While the Shakers and early Quakers cannot be called 'universalists' in the reconciliatory sense, their religious views were nonetheless more socially inclusive than those of many mainstream and orthodox religions. Like the French Prophets, the Shakers and early Quakers shared a deep sense of religious conviction continually fuelled by the persecution they had to endure, but their unwavering beliefs united members of the groups while attracting new converts. Their simple ways were the outward expression of a deep-seated inner simplicity, which could be extended to all, they believed.

In 1772, two years almost to the day before Ann Lee left England for America, an American arrived in England with intentions similar to Mother Ann's: to profess the virtues of simple living and universal love. His name was John Woolman; he was a Quaker. The journal he left behind is possibly one of the most compelling accounts of simple living in the eighteenth century in North America and beyond. While the Shakers did not trace their steps back to Manchester once their communities were established in the New World, the Quakers, or Friends as they referred to themselves, crossed the Atlantic back and forth. Elizabeth Hooton, who with George Fox had the first 'quaking' experience in late 1646 or early 1647, travelled to the Americas three times before she died in Jamaica in 1672. In New England, where she visited twice, the Puritans' whip did not crack her religious convictions. William Penn, who had converted to Quakerism in 1666, founded Philadelphia, the City of Brotherly Love, in 1682. He too travelled back to England two years later before finally returning to Pennsylvania in 1699. In the meantime, his dream of a Quaker city did not materialize. For the Quakers and Shakers, and much like the Puritans before them, the New World offered opportunities to create new societies with simple living, plainness and humility as core values. Of all three groups, the Shakers, probably because of their partial retreat from the world, preserved their simple ways of life, although with constant vigilance and a certain rigour. But all three sects went through a period when scores of members traded simplicity for worldlier gains. The growing number of apostates abandoning their simple ways provoked indignation and triggered concerted reactions in Quaker and Shaker communities. In response to the corruption of conscience by easy money, staunch believers professed to their neighbours, close and far, their loyalty to simplicity as a core religious and social virtue as well as a way of life.

Quakerism started in the Midlands, England, in 1646 or 1647. Quakers believed in a divine presence or 'inward light' in all. They were accused of antinomianism for their questioning of clerical and civil authorities and they suffered brutal persecution for the trust they placed in the 'inward light' rather than in the Scriptures. Early Quakers were also known for their religious and civil disobedience. Friends would disrupt orthodox religious services with all the vigour granted by unwavering religious conviction. They objected to the 'hat honour' or habit of doffing one's hat in the presence of someone of higher rank. By this, they signalled that all men and women are born equal. They would speak plainly, addressing all with a plain 'thou', regardless of rank or dignity. Their public persecutions and judgements were on a par with the perceived severity of the crimes they committed against established religion. One Friend who was to suffer the wrath of religious authorities was James Nayler, who had the 'B' for blasphemy branded on his forehead after entering Bristol on Palm Sunday in the manner in which Christ entered Jerusalem.

With George Fox, James Nayler was one of the main spiritual guides of early Quakerism, although he was controversial within the sect. Even before he was imprisoned and tortured for blasphemy, Nayler was revered by his followers as the new Christ, as the One who walked the way of simplicity. To his fellow Quakers he wrote the following aphorism: 'The Lord God of Peace Rebuke him, who daily seeks to turn the Simplicity out of its Way.'[24] For Nayler, the erring believer is prey to the Devil, who beguiles Man of the life of simplicity. The unsimple Man becomes the servant of lust and 'self-ended things'.[25] 'The Serpent being above upon the Earth, seeks to catch into the Imaginations, and the Creature being led to consult with him there, in the Flesh, he beguiles the Creature of the *Simplicity*, and so keeps the Creature in self,' wrote Nayler in plain yet vibrant prose.[26] This passage shows that for Nayler, simplicity is the ferment of selflessness; it is dispensed by God to individual consciences but it is always under the threat of the Serpent, the one who beguiles, deceives and divides. The Serpent symbolizes duplicity, or the division of the self. The divided self is locked 'in self', self-absorbed as it is, and is only preoccupied with 'self-ended things'. Hence the fear expressed by Nayler in a letter to a Friend: 'Truly my Heart dreads for fear of more Divisions.'[27] Divisions are the work of the Devil. 'But that which leads into the Simplicity of Life, which is manifest in the Spirit, and not in the Knowledge of the first Man, that leads to the Resurrection of Life' is good.[28] Simplicity is not the buttressed wall erected around an invincible inner fortress called the self; it is life, resurrection and true spiritual abundance. Those who 'have suffered the Simplicity to be deceived . . . are led back to the old beggarly rudiments of the World again.'[29] The price of deception is steep: it is poverty, spiritual poverty, the kind that remains invisible to the deceived, who is too occupied with the veil of riches that covers his gaping paucity of spirit. What is paramount for Nayler is vigilance against the many deceits eating away at simplicity and simple people. Some will let the simplicity of the Word be 'deceived with Meanings, Addings, and Wrestings', all distortions and unnecessary supplements corrupting the simple truth of the Gospel.[30] Nayler's warning may still ring true: 'Now these are the perilous Times, wherein Simplicity is taken in the Snares of Subtilty [*sic*].'[31] Subtlety or that which does not speak of itself is the sign that the end is nigh. And in the sound and the fury of undecipherable signs, the 'still, small voice' of God cannot be heard. Simplicity is the silence of consciousness readying itself to hear the quiet murmurs of the divine.

For William Penn, early Christians lived simply because they were capable of 'receiving the Simplicity of the Gospel', rendering them impervious to a 'Pride in false Knowledge', to lies and the illusions of riches.[32] Although some seventeenth-century Quakers still dressed in plain clothes in the imitation of early Christians, who 'minded them for Covering', for many Friends, as Penn laments, covering 'is the least Part'.[33] Wantonness, pleasure, 'gaudy Superfluities' are in fashion, 'as if they made their Clothes for Trimming, to be seen rather than worn'.[34] Penn's initial concern with superfluity, excess and vanity, all enemies of simplicity and plainness, turns into outrage when he addresses yet another form of waste: when early Christians engaged in recreations it was 'to serve God, be just, follow their Vocations, mind their Flocks, do Good, exercise their Bodies in such Manner as was suitable to Gravity, Temperance and Virtue'.[35] In William Penn's view, recreations are so divorced from necessity and virtue that, while they are pleasing amusements in the moment, they hardly rise above the level of 'scandalous filth', leaving us with a feeling of repugnance when they are over. Penn's words are clear:

How ignoble is it! how ignominious and unworthy of a reasonable Creature; Man which is endued with Understanding, fit to contemplate Immortality, and made a Companion (if not Superior) to Angels, that he should mind a little Dust, a few shameful Rags; Inventions of mere Pride and Luxury; Toys, so apish and fantastick; Entertainments so dull and earthy, that a Rattle, a Baby, a Hobby-horse, a Top, are by no Means so Foolish in a simple Child, nor unworthy of his Thoughts, as are such Inventions of the Care and Pleasure of Men. It is a Mark of great Stupidity that such Vanities should exercise the noble Mind of Man, and Image of the great Creator of the Heaven and Earth.[36]

A man acting, thinking and feeling like a simple child, or even an ape, is wasting his God-given abilities. The nobility of man resides in the appropriate use of his faculties. Being simple and living simply mean using one's resources wisely, sparingly and aptly. Penn railed against frivolous habits and puerile recreations because they are not worthy of reasonable beings. His demanding Rationalist humanism did not speak to all Friends in Pennsylvania and England. The pull of riches was great. George Fox's and William Penn's contempt for merchants, luxury and the exploitation of peasants was no secret. But forsaking wealth tests one's convictions, and some Friends thought twice before relinquishing their fortunes. Many Quakers rejected strict admonitions and saw excesses in simplicity as condemnable as superfluity. Robert Barclay is one example. His *Apology for the True Christian Divinity* (1676) takes aim at some of the sterner reprimands found in conservative Quaker writings. One such example is his treatment of recreations, which were vilified as unsimple by some traditionalist Friends. About plays he asked: 'How many *idle words* do they necessarily produce? Yea, what are *comedies* but a *studied complex of idle and lying words?*[37] According to Barclay, a play will produce idle and lying words – words, therefore, which are anything but simple. He describes comedy as a 'studied complex.' Here 'studied' means unnatural and 'complex' means unsimple, a double negative rendering the full deleterious effect of theatre. Despite his admonitions against such activities, Barclay concedes that if they are aligned with the right intentions, these recreations can be acceptable and indeed beneficial. The mind needs relaxation from virtuous occupations, and so does the 'outward man', or physical man, from righteous travails. But such relaxation shall not be superfluous, licentious, vain or wanton, writes Barclay.[38] In trying to gauge what is too much simplicity in clothing, recreation and wealth, Barclay was posing questions that may well be insoluble: what is too simple? Is simplicity a moveable goalpost, relocated with every occasion? Relativizing simplicity also meant questioning its universality, durability and possibly its very essence.

For some Friends, the testimony of simplicity meant they had to renounce lucrative businesses and profitable occupations that would have distracted them from achieving greatness in Christ. For some the trading and enslaving of other human beings and the violence exercised against all living beings in the name of profit could not be justified. Two figures stand out among the many Friends who opposed greed, violence and slavery. One was Benjamin Lay, a dwarf who was a fierce and boisterous abolitionist. The other was a poised and soft-spoken man who, as mentioned above, wrote one of the most inspiring journals: John Woolman. Their values were similar; their ways were different.

From an upsetting experience early in his life, John Woolman learnt that there resides in all of us an inalienable principle of goodness that guides us to care for all living creatures. His life was the life of the 'quietest radical in history', according to Quaker historian Frederick Tolles.[39] His voice was 'still and small', but his message of simplicity, peace, justice and equality was heard by many. John Woolman ran a successful tailor's shop, and in his own words he was a born trader. But the embarrassment of riches, the impulse to expand in order to sell ever more, contradicted the principle of simplicity that he had spiritually, intellectually and physically endorsed. To live simply, he decided to renounce his business ventures and riches and instead to dedicate his life to pursuits of a more altruistic kind. He advocated for the poor, for slaves and for multitudes of voiceless human and non-human beings. Having heard that the living and working conditions in English mills were dire, he left America for England in the hope of alleviating the suffering of the victims of the Industrial Revolution by preaching a civil gospel of simple living, kindness and respect. A couple of months before his death in Yorkshire – he was never to return to America – he had a dream in which he saw a 'mass of matter of a dull and gloomy color' representing the whole of humankind in its misery; he knew that he was not a 'distinct or separate being' and that his lot was to improve theirs. His *Plea for the Poor*, published posthumously in 1793, is a written testament of the 'duty of tenderness' towards the poor and all those in need, those working to enrich others, these poor men and women eking out a living in horrendous conditions by manufacturing superfluous goods that would enslave the minds of others. His quiet radicalism bore no sign of paternalism or condescension. Where Christ's love extended to all beings, so did his.

> As by his breath the flame of life was kindled in all animal
> sensible creatures, to say we love God as unseen, and at

the same time exercise cruelty toward the least creature moving by his life, or by life derived from him, was a contradiction in itself. I found no narrowness respecting sects and opinions, but believed that sincere, upright-hearted people, in every society, who truly love God, were accepted of him.

As I lived under the cross, and simply followed the opening of truth, my mind, from day to day, was more enlightened . . . My heart was tender and often contrite, and universal love to my fellow-creatures increased in me.[40]

This passage synthesizes John Woolman's way. He loved all creatures and his personal enlightenment hailed from what he called 'the opening of truth': exposing internal contradictions, which fuel injustices of all sorts, to reveal the truth. One of the greatest contradictions is to love God while hating creatures whose lives spring from Him. He explained:

I believe where the love of God is verily perfected, and the true spirit of government watchfully attended to, a tenderness towards all creatures made subject to us will be experienced, and a care felt in us that we do not lessen that sweetness of life in the animal creation which the great Creator intends for them under our government.[41]

For Woolman, the duty of tenderness and duty of care are the bedrocks of government, civil and domestic, and of all interactions between humans and animals. It is in this context of a universal ethics of care that simplicity is lodged:

Remember, O my soul! That the Prince of Peace is thy
Lord; that he communicates his unmixed wisdom to his
family, that they, living in perfect simplicity, may give no
just cause of offense to any creature, but that they may
walk as He walked![42]

The simplicity that John Woolman is advocating is the practice
of tenderness in all matters of the heart, mind and body and
towards all beings. Simplicity as tenderness is not only an emo-
tion flooding the world and washing away injustice, inequalities
and contradictions; it is the motivation of all actions. Perfect
simplicity is simplicity manifest in small and great deeds. It is
also a vigilance that such deeds should satisfy virtues of justice
and equality for all beings. Small deeds such as rejecting blue
clothes because the indigo dye was produced by slaves or walking
instead of horse riding so as not to hurt horses. Great deeds such
as confronting Quaker slave-owners with the cruelty they inflict
on others; great deeds in crossing the Atlantic to defend the basic
rights of indentured mill workers in England.

John Woolman shared such aspirations with other Quakers
of his generation. One of his contemporaries, Anthony Benezet,
born Antoine Bénézet to a French Protestant family, converted
to Quakerism in 1727 and emigrated to Philadelphia four years
later. Benezet was a staunch abolitionist and a born educator.
He founded his own schools, the first public school for girls
in America, and a school for black children, as well as the first
abolitionist society, the Society for the Relief of Free Negroes
Unlawfully Held in Bondage. Anthony Benezet witnessed the erosion of many Friends' religious convictions, lost to the trappings
of the world and the promises of riches. One reaction against

the dilution of commitment to foundational values such as simplicity took the form of militant Quietism, inspired by Catholic mystics. Like other Quietist Quakers, Benezet insisted on humility and purity as well as the passive receptiveness of the will of God. They also placed great emphasis on communal holiness and detachment from the seductions of the world. Benezet was the author of *Observations on Plainness and Simplicity in Conduct and Conversation*, a short pamphlet reasserting the importance of plain speech and plain dress as true Quaker principles. For him, Quakers who err from simplicity and plainness not only betray Quaker principles, they also betray non-Quakers, who had come to expect simplicity in all the actions and manners of the Friends. Simplicity is the exterior sign of Quakerism, a sign that separates Quakers from the World and unites them in a community of kindred plain spirits.[43] For the Quietist Quaker, the promise of simple living is to 'overcome the world'.[44] 'Be not discouraged, dear young Friends,' writes Benezet, 'you who have seen the necessity of taking up the cross in your dress and address, and have, in some degree, yielded obedience thereto.'[45] His advice to the younger generation was to bear the Cross of Christ, the cross of simplicity, inside and outside.

In the latter part of the eighteenth century, Elias Hicks, whose convictions adhered to the main precepts of Quietist Quakerism, created a great division among the Friends. For Hicks, the Quakers would do better to imitate the moral exemplarity of Christ rather than pontificate on his divinity. Hicksites, followers of Hicks, also advocated humility and patience. Hicks's journal warns against the loss of simplicity and purity as primary values of the Quakers' 'holy self-denying profession'; simplicity through exercise and travail is for Hicks and his flock the sign and practice of the separation from the world and the condition for the arising of a new life.[46] His journal reads like a lamentation on the many departures from simple living he observes among the Friends, especially the younger ones. He writes of the 'apostacy from primitive simplicity.'[47] The 26 December 1813 entry of his journal relates a particularly memorable meeting that was dominated by simplicity. He writes:

> Sat the greater part of our meeting in much weakness and poverty of spirit, to which I felt perfectly resigned, believing it to be agreeable to the Lord's will. But towards the close an honest elderly Friend, though young and small in such service, expressed a sentence or two accompanied with a degree of life, which seemed to give spring to a concern on my mind, which led to communication. The subject which opened to show, that plainness and simplicity were the true marks and badges of the Lord's people and children in every age of the world, witnessed to by the true nature and analogy of all things in the universe; and confirmed by the testimony of the grace and good spirit of God through his servants in all the generations of mankind.[48]

This moment is particularly important as it captures two qualities of simplicity. The first is poverty of spirit, willed by God and experienced by Hicks in obliging passivity. Only the poor and simple in spirit, who are humbly conscious of their poverty or want, will seek spiritual riches in God; those who do not see their own spiritual poverty will desperately accumulate material riches of no lasting value. 'Blessed are the poor in spirit, for theirs is the Kingdom of Heaven' is the first beatitude proclaimed by Jesus in his 'Sermon on the Mount'. The second quality of simplicity enunciated in the experience reported in Hicks's journal is indelibility. Simplicity is the mark of God in all His creatures. That mark is permanent, universal and unequivocal. In Hicks's journal, simplicity is spiritual want, divine sign, pure absence and eternal presence. With such an idealization of simplicity, perhaps it is no wonder that few could endorse it and that only primitive Christians, or the idea he had of them, could be wholeheartedly simple and plain in dress, address, mind and spirit. Until his last days, he lamented the departure from simplicity in younger generations. In *The Memorial of Jericho Monthly Meeting of Friends Concerning Our Ancient Friend Elias Hicks*, one reads that at the end of his life he was troubled by the many 'deviations from that plainness and simplicity into which the truth would lead; he expressed the comfort it would be to him to see a reformation in these respects'.[49] Hicks's simplicity is not for the faint of heart: it does not lead to truth, but truth leads to it; it is not a midpoint between the here and now and higher goals such as truth, the Holy Grail of many belief systems. Simplicity is that Holy Grail.

Such an idealization of simplicity and plainness, perhaps more present in primitive Quakerism and the Hicksites' writings than in other Friends' texts, was not the norm. Simplicity was for many Quakers a matter of dress and address motivated by solid ideas of social justice and egalitarianism. The testimony of simplicity has over the years been absorbed into other causes and professions of Quaker beliefs such as voluntary poverty, sustainability and justice for all. From the early years in the seventeenth century, the Children of the Light, as Quakers called themselves then, were vocal and resolute, not afraid of disrupting Anglican services to publicly show their dissent. One such way for early Quakers to protest the untruths of orthodox religions was 'walking naked' in public in the image of the Prophet Isaiah. In 1652 George Fox wrote: 'The Lord made one to go naked among you, a figure of thy nakedness, and of your nakedness, and as a sign amongst you before your destruction cometh, that you might see that you were naked and not covered with the truth.'[50]

In the 1650s and early 1660s, many Friends stripped off their worldly garb to show others their own nudity, a nudity that no superfluous attire could cover. In the absence of a written creed, Quakers taught by *signs* such as nakedness, or sackcloth for their only clothing, or covering the body with ashes. William Craig Brownlee, a Presbyterian pastor and scholar who had little affection for the Friends, was quick to assimilate nude protestation to the long tradition of defiant nakedness, from the Greek Cynic Diogenes to the medieval French Turlupins, whose nudism was the genuine profession of their vow of poverty.[51] The association between Quakerism and Cynicism was realized in the eighteenth century when pioneering abolitionist Benjamin Lay shocked an assembly of Friends with a spectacular dissenting act. On 19 September 1738, at a Quaker Meeting in Burlington, New Jersey, he hid an animal bladder filled with pokeberry juice into a hollowed-out Bible. Having vigorously condemned slavery in front of the assembly, he raised the Bible above his head and pierced the Holy Book with a sword, spilling the blood-coloured juice on himself and those around him as he shouted 'Thus shall God shed the blood of those persons who enslave their fellow creatures.'[52] Such demonstrations testify to the turbulent spirit of their author; they also show the force of his convictions and the risks he was willing to take to come to the defence of others. A recent biographer described him as a 'class-conscious, gender-conscious, race-conscious, environmentally conscious vegetarian radical.'[53] All the epithets apply. His simplicity was at once dramatic and genuine, in the manner of the Greek Cynic philosopher to whom he was compared, notably by Benjamin Franklin. In the *Pennsylvania Gazette* dated 25 March 1742, Lay was described as a 'Pythagorean-cynical-christian Philosopher.'[54] In 1746 a New Jersey politician dubbed him a 'Comi-Cynic Philosopher.'[55]

FOUR

A SIMPLE REFORM

'Diogenes' monkey' was the name Voltaire gave to Jean-Jacques Rousseau. For Kant, however, he was the 'sublime Diogenes'. The monikers may divulge Voltaire's and Kant's own views on Rousseau's philosophical project, but they fail to capture his ideas. Truth be told, the Genevan philosopher, like the Greek Cynic before him, decided at one point to simplify his life. In fact, he started his philosophical career with a sudden simplification of his ways, a transformation that he called his 'reform'. As his fame as a writer and philosopher grew in his early forties, he honoured a promise he had made to himself when he was younger:

From the time of my youth, I had set this age of forty as the terminal point for my efforts to succeed and as the one for all of my vain ambitions . . . I was fully resolved once this age was reached that whatever situation I might be in, I would struggle no longer to get out of it and would spend the remainder of my days living from day to day without ever concerning myself about the future . . . In releasing myself from all those lures and vain hopes, I fully gave myself up to carelessness and to the peace of mind

which always constituted my most dominant pleasure
and most lasting propensity. I forsook the world and its
pomp; I renounced all finery: no more sword, no more
watch, no more white stockings, gilding, or head-dress;
a very simple wig, a good coarse cloth garment . . . I did
not restrict my reform to external things . . . I undertook
to submit my inner self to a severe examination.[1]

A simpler appearance, the rejection of symbols of nobility like
the sword, the reliance on the moment rather than on conventional measurements of time, as well as a deep introspection
– these practices buttress the edifice of Rousseau's philosophy.
That alone does not make him a Cynic. For one thing he was
very much attached to his reputation and he was still wearing a
wig, a simple one to be sure, but a wig nonetheless. If others saw
a Cynic in him, Rousseau himself did not. The fictional judge
in his autobiographical *Dialogues*, pronouncing on the philosopher's simplicity – was it real or mere affectation? – and on his
alleged Cynicism, declared that Jean-Jacques' simplicity was not
faked and that he was not a copycat of the best-known Cynic.[2]
Diogenes was Diogenes; Rousseau had to be the best Rousseau
he could be without impersonating someone else and shattering
his sense of self.

Jean-Jacques Rousseau has long been associated with the
idea of a return to nature. After the publication of his incendi-
ary *Discourse on the Origins of Inequality* in 1755, he was accused
by his enemies, chief among them Voltaire, of advocating naive
primitivism. Those who had read him superficially had seen in
his writings an exhortation to walk on all fours like an animal,
an appeal to return to nature – not just to a simpler way of living

but a regression to a non-human state. Herein lies the misunderstanding. Rousseau never encouraged anyone to return to nature, to live in the woods, or to relapse to some primitive Golden Age. His 'state of nature' is hypothetical, a heuristic device for conveying his ideas on humankind, history and the world. He wrote that the state of nature does not exist, perhaps never existed, and will probably never exist.[3] It is a merely hypothetical standard against which to measure our life goals, our societies, our hopes and ourselves. There is in fact no real state of nature, present or past, to return to, and no naive glorification of primitivism in his oeuvre.

In the spring of 1764, a woman using the pseudonym Henriette wrote to Rousseau for advice. She had fallen into misfortune and suffered from what we would today call severe depression. Henriette found solace in literature and philosophy and had become an avid reader of Rousseau's texts. When reading *Emile*, in which the philosopher set forth his views on education and human nature, she came upon a passage that prompted her to write to him. In this book, Rousseau expressed the opinion, not uncommon at this time, that a woman's knowledge should be limited to child-rearing and the household and should exclude such futile refinements as belles-lettres. 'I would still like a simple and coarsely raised girl a hundred times better than a learned and brilliant one,' proclaims Emile's mentor.[4] These are the words Henriette read. For Emile's teacher, a simple woman is a woman whose 'dignity consists in being ignored', who knows her place and her 'natural' tasks.[5] In her letter, Henriette asked Rousseau whether exceptions could be made, whether a woman could read philosophy, especially when philosophy might bring consolation to a soul as troubled as hers. The philosopher's response was not encouraging:

Let us first discard useless deliberations. It is not a matter of reducing you to sewing and embroidering, Henriette; one does not remove one's head as one removes one's hat, and one does not return to simplicity or childhood; once the mind is activated, it stays active, and whoever had a thought will always have thoughts . . . let's not talk about changing condition, but making the most of yours.[6]

Rousseau counsels his devotee to adapt to her new circumstances and use them to her advantage. The therapeutic and philosophical values of such recommendations are questionable; what mattered for Rousseau and what his detractors failed to see, intentionally or not, is that progress and change are inevitable but are largely outside of our control, that there is no possible return to simplicity, whether of a child or of a long past Golden Age, once the individual mind is activated and once societies are engaged in progress, whether scientific, social, political or artistic. Henriette had to find a way to put her knowledge of philosophy and her actuated mind to good use. Her first decision, as she wrote to Rousseau, was to 'return to nature and simplicity'.[7] This was not some vague, original simplicity, which is irretrievable, but a simplicity of duty towards oneself and others, the pleasure felt not in things but in good deeds. Having retreated to the countryside, Henriette discovered that she did not need 'vain and noisy pleasures, the simplest are enough'.[8] In Rousseau's letters, and more importantly in her own experiences, Henriette learnt that she should not suspend the activities of her life trying to become who she was not; on the contrary, she should, like all of us, strive to become the best she could possibly be. Our duty consists, then, in perfecting ourselves rather than in impeding our natural perfectibility with illusory pleasures and useless activities. If original simplicity is a myth with heuristic value, the thoughtful, thorough and authentic simplification of our lives enables our natural perfectibility to flourish. This is the first lesson.

Perfectibility is an important concept for Rousseau. Like progress, it is inevitable. The faculty of perfecting oneself is a specifically human trait. Whereas animals reach their developmental endpoint within a few months, humans continue to change throughout their lives and in changing move away from what they once were, both as individuals and as members of societies. Perfectibility is neither good nor bad. It has inspired some of the greatest human inventions, but it also turned man into 'the tyrant of himself and of Nature'.[9] Although hypothetical, Rousseau's history is somewhat prophetic. His ambition in his *Discourse on the Origins of Inequality* was to analyse with surgical precision the natural and the societal in man.

The task Rousseau took upon himself consisted in stripping man of the unnatural and supplementary traits he had acquired since he left the state of nature. He hoped to paint the portrait, fictitious yet inspirational and heuristic, of natural man. Rousseau's hypothetical history is divided into five main ages. In the first age or state of nature, man, governed by his sensations, lived alone in a bountiful natural environment providing for all his wants. Natural man lived in complete autarchy, concerned only with satisfying his natural needs and occupied only with himself. The second age saw the first encounters of individuals with the nascent virtues like prudence, a quality necessary for mitigating interpersonal relations. In the third age, language appeared along with moral laws, and also private property, and with them inequality and war. In the 'policed' or fourth age, nations, love, merit and beauty appeared. The final age, or age of letters, corresponds to our own decadent times.[10] These ages are not neatly separated; they are like strata with blurred junctures which all together compose a whole.

In the first age natural man is physiologically similar to modern man. He has no simian attributes, but is simply man yet unaltered by civilization, displaying traits we seem to have lost over the course of human history. To discover natural man, Rousseau proceeds by subtraction:

> Stripping this Being, so constituted, of all the supernatural gifts he could have received and of all the artificial faculties he could only have acquired by long progress – considering him, in a word, as he must have come from the hands of Nature – I see an animal less strong than some, less agile than others, but all things considered, the most advantageously organized of all. I see him satisfying his hunger under an oak, quenching his thirst at the first Stream, finding his bed at the foot of the same tree that furnished his meal; and therewith his needs are satisfied.

> The Earth, abandoned to its natural fertility and covered by immense forests never mutilated by the Axe, offers at every step Store-houses and shelters of animals of all species.[11]

First, a word on the 'natural fertility' of the earth. In a note related to this passage and inspired by Buffon's *Natural History*, Rousseau attributes the destruction of the soil to its over-cultivation.[12] Not to paint him as an early modern advocate of sustainability, but his idea that the exhaustion of resources results from their overuse agrees with the notion that nature gives freely while man takes freely and carelessly, never moderating his needs and desires. In the same way, man observed, imitated and freely appropriated animals' instincts; from these he developed a panoply of adopted faculties and talents when he had none originally.[13] All of this was fine until men teamed up into social groups.

This painting of the state of nature, bucolic as it may be, reveals Rousseau's method: to remove the add-ons, the supernatural and the artificial – any unnecessary supplement layered upon natural man after he left the state of nature and entered history, so to speak, and created societies. Beneath the layers lies a fictitious being whose creator had endowed him with 'heavenly and majestic simplicity', a being 'acting always by fixed and invariable principles'.[14] Natural man is simple and predictable.

With the passage of time, with progress – the by-product of perfectibility – and changes of all types, 'how will man manage to see himself as Nature formed him'? asks Rousseau.[15] To identify modifications in us, the inquisitive mind must remember that *social man* is the sum of changes, some imposed on us by Nature, others forced upon us by none other than ourselves. Natural man, or as Rousseau calls him, *simple man*, is a benchmark of a sort against which we can gauge our changes, our progress and our deviances from simple intentions and needs. For Rousseau, being simple, acting simply and thinking simply are not the privileges of the few who have retreated from the world to live in the desert or within the walls of monasteries. Simplicity is an intellectual and moral imperative of self-evaluation and permanent moral reassessment, so that we are neither our own tyrants nor the tyrants of nature. To know oneself, to catch a glimpse of the simple man in oneself, is not self-absorption or withdrawal within oneself; it is a necessary exercise that may benefit man, society and nature. Paradoxically, to fail to examine oneself is to go about life blindly and credulously.

For Rousseau, civil society has a clear starting point: 'the first person who, having fenced off a plot of land, took it into his head to say *this is mine* and found people simple enough to believe him, was the true founder of civil society.'[16] This excerpt from his *Discourse on the Origins of Inequality* shows society as beginning with one man forcibly taking possession of land, claiming that it was his, and meeting with no opposition from his fellows. Civil society is founded on an illegitimate appropriation, a unilateral declaration of possession and a tacit agreement by all expropriated to say nothing, to do nothing. The annexation is unpunished because those present at the time were simple enough to be duped by the words 'this is mine.' To survive as a myth, the idea of property requires the gullibility or simplicity of the dispossessed. Ownership and civil society are the products of a usurpation of common land and of common sense ratified by simple people.

In his *Political Fragments*, Rousseau noted that conniving politicians and men of unscrupulous morals misused reason and rhetoric to profit from the 'credulity of the simple-minded'.[17] The deception of simple people has infected all aspects of society since that fateful pronouncement, 'this is mine.' No moral judgement should be ascribed to the appellation 'simple people' as Rousseau intends it. It is a provocation on the part of the philosopher who is presenting a mirror to his readers, and to the lies they are fed – readers who are complicit because they are simple. Simplicity as gullibility is not a natural trait but a complacency and a wilful ignorance. Here is the paradox and the good news: the deception can be reversed by simple people themselves if they overturn the decision to accept everything at face value.

How can simple people rebel against annexation, usurpation, grand theft and duplicity? A revolutionary return to a state of harmony with nature and simplicity seems out of the realm of possibility for those who have left the state of nature. Only *simple man* can exist in the state of original simplicity, and even that is more an idea than a historical fact. You leave nature and you lose it. What about 'men like me, whose passions have forever destroyed their original simplicity, who can no longer nourish themselves on grass and nuts, nor do without Laws or Chiefs?' asks Rousseau.[18] The answer is similar to the one he gave to Henriette. One cannot return to the past, but one can work to improve the current situation and build a more just society. To that end, those who believe in the supernatural should base their actions on sound moral principles dictated by their faith. All should respect and obey just governments but show contempt for governments from which 'arise more real calamities than apparent advantages'.[19] Once in civil society, a man can no longer be uncritical and simple-minded – that is, gullible – as the intentions of others generally contradict his, while his own intentions are often tainted by his own passions, including the desire to have what others own.

But not all is lost; civil simplicity is a virtue to endorse and cultivate as it can spawn better societies and people:

> As long as several men together consider themselves to be a single body, they have only a single will, which relates to their common preservation and the general welfare. Then all of the mechanisms of the State are vigorous and simple, its maxims are clear and luminous, it has no tangled, contradictory interests; the common good is clearly

apparent everywhere, and requires only good sense to be perceived. Peace, union, and equality are enemies of political subtleties. *Upright and simple men are hard to fool because of their simplicity*; traps and refined pretexts do not deceive them. They are not even clever enough to be duped. When, among the happiest people in the world, groups of peasants are seen deciding the affairs of State under an oak, and always acting wisely, can one help scorning the refinements of other nations, which make themselves illustrious and miserable with so much art and mystery?[20]

Simplicity in this passage appears under a different light. First there is the simplicity or singleness of the general will, a concept dear to Rousseau. The general will is not the sum of private wills. Private wills are governed by principles of self-interest, including self-preservation. Although positive and productive, private wills can also enter into a war between different personal interests and passions. Private wills breed division. The general will is not the aggregate of these belligerent private wills; it is the victory over private wills and the assimilation of private wills into one general will, which seeks not just the satisfaction and preservation of the self, but the satisfaction and preservation of all. Although they are moved by a similar principle, the two wills differ on one fundamental level: private will is divisive, pitting personal interests against personal interests; general will is inclusive to the extent that private wills are not identifiable but absorbed within the general will, which is one. This sovereign authority or general will is simple, 'single and unique, and cannot be divided without being destroyed'.[21]

A government issued from the simplicity of the general will would be simple. And for Rousseau, 'simple Government is the best in itself, by the very fact that it is simple.'[22] But he quickly concedes that 'properly speaking, there is no simple Government' because power is distributed between several agents or institutions.[23] Government will consist in moderating the many private wills and the simple general will in contractual arrangements beneficial to the greatest number of citizens. To govern is to balance the simple and the many. When the latter is composed of the smallest number of particulars or individuals, it is easier to moderate between the one and the multiple. Republics with the smallest populations have simpler governments and the 'mechanisms of the State' are simpler.

When the general will is sovereign, the simplicity of the instruments of the State are transparent to all and explicable by all, as all take part in it and give rise to it. Interests are in accord and common sense prevails. Simple men cannot be deceived by political rhetoric because of their simplicity, writes Rousseau. The tautology is surprising only if one forgets that simple people are not clever enough to be duped. By 'clever' Rousseau means prone or susceptible to refinement, finery, sophistry and excesses in everything, which create a chain reaction of division and atomization. The simplicity of simple people is a force for unity, not separation.

For Rousseau, the distance between people, objects and words leaves room for manipulations and verbal treachery. Distance is created between individuals, and in that space between you and me all manner of tensions provoked by our private wills may arise. The proximity between oneself and others and a sense of closeness and familiarity with one's environment is the privilege of simple people. A simple soul, as Claire wrote to Julie in Rousseau's novel, is one 'who seeks only, so to speak, to latch onto what surrounds you.'[24] The villagers in the novel live a simple life, with simple mores and tastes. They only concern themselves with people and objects within their immediate physical and moral reach. The novel turns into an ode to simplicity, an *apologia* for simple living.

In the state of nature, man roams the countryside alone, facing dangers alone. He develops rudimentary skills to survive. In this condition natural man is strong compared to social man, who overeats refined foods, which cause inflammations and ills no doctor can cure. Rousseau lists a variety of assaults against social man's physical and mental health, the worst being suffered by the poor, because social and economic inequality brings inequality in health. Social man cannot control his desires, he suffers from 'fatigues and exhaustions of Mind' and the many sorrows that erode his soul.[25] His conclusion: 'These are the fatal proofs that most of our ills are our own work, and that we would have avoided almost all of them by preserving the simple, uniform and solitary way of life prescribed to us by Nature.'[26]

This state of perfect simplicity, uniformity and solitude does not survive the first associations between men, which over time generate such passions as envy, pride and violence. In an early version of the *Social Contract*, Rousseau described the passage from the perfect state of nature to a new, transitional order, which is not yet civil society nor a 'policed' society:

This new order of things gives rise to a multitude of relationships without lacking order, regulation, and stability, which men alter and change continually – a hundred working to destroy them for one working to establish them. And since the relative existence of a man in the state of nature is dependent on a thousand other constantly changing relationships, he can never make sure of being the same for two moments in his life.[27]

Society, even in its embryonic form, begets complexity. The ailments this man suffers from are also ours. And for Rousseau the worst of all is the lost capacity to be oneself, as one: constancy of self is lost with the advent of society. What is gained, though, is the capacity to learn about oneself and others, if only in order to survive in a constantly changing world.

As Louis Althusser has shown, the state of nature according to Rousseau is not constitutive of a causality; it is not an origin, although it contains, in embryonic form, certain conditions of socialization such as pity.[28] Like the state of nature, which is ahistorical but ever present, so is simplicity. For Rousseau, the simplicity that counts serves as a remedy against the poisonous effects of denaturation and over-socialization. Simplicity for social man is not a gift; it is not retrieved from an original state; it is acquired and practised, and it is even taught.

The education of Emile in Rousseau's eponymous book is one in which the distinction between living and making a living is first experienced by the student and then explained by the mentor. Learning to live a life is learning to adapt to all situations; learning to make a living is training for a profession, which will leave you helpless in situations where your specialist skills and knowledge will prove incomplete or inadequate. Rousseau captures this idea in the following formula: 'Happy is the man who knows how to leave the station which leaves him and to remain a man in spite of fate.'[29] Conditions change, situations are in flux, societies mutate and so does man, caught up in the denaturing process of history. A happy man who lives his life to the fullest is one who does not cling to what passes; he is the one who lets go and goes on. There still remains one natural and simple principle that animates all people: the preservation of life. According to Rousseau: 'The principles according to which the virtuous man learns to despise his life and to sacrifice it to his duty are very far from this primitive simplicity. Happy are the peoples among whom one can be good without effort and just without virtue!'[30]

It is within communities of people living their lives, not just making a living, that one can live simply, effortlessly and fully. In societies where people's ambitions amount to making a good living, being good is a duty, an effort. The virtuous man is the man of man; he is the man who labours at being a good man for the sake of living in the society of men and fostering social ties with his fellows. The man of nature is neither industrious nor virtuous: he is simply living in simplicity. 'I valued modesty and honesty; I was happy cultivating them in a simple and laborious life,' wrote Julie to her suitor.[31] Here is the best scenario: living a simple and laborious life surrounded by simple and laborious people who know themselves well and who know each other well. Today, simplicity has become a virtue, an effort. But what kind of a virtue is it?

Two men, both paragons of simplicity, are selected by Rousseau's vicar in *Emile* to explain the true nature of virtue: Socrates, the philosopher, and Christ, the simplest of all men. Socrates, hailed as the father of philosophy and as a beacon of moral rectitude until his death, does not compare to Christ, according to the vicar. The Greek philosopher had merely put the actions of great men into words. 'Before he had defined virtue, Greece abounded in virtuous men,' writes Rousseau.[32] Even his death by poison, surrounded by his followers, had been peaceful, easy and almost enviable. This scene of serene passing has nothing in common with the crucifixion, when Jesus suffered the insults and violence of his captors, whom he forgave as he expired. More importantly still, Christ did not define virtue by copying the virtuous actions of others who came before him. No one before him, writes the vicar, had been as virtuous as he. He had no example to follow; he *was* the example. 'From the womb of the most furious fanaticism was heard the highest wisdom, and the simplicity of the most heroic virtue lent honor to the vilest of all peoples.'[33] Interestingly, it is not virtues that lend honour, it is the simplicity of the virtue that cast honour on even the 'vilest of all peoples'. The simplicity of virtue is not only virtue in its purest form. A virtue is simple if there is no such virtue before it, if there is no virtuous model to emulate, define or philosophize on. A virtuous act is simple if it is not a replica, or a lesson passively learnt and applied. Second-hand virtues and learned virtuous acts are necessary, but they are not simple; they are duplicates and fruits of labour.

We know that the idea of origin is fraught in Rousseau. Origin is neither causal nor historical; it is separated from history by an accident:

> After having shown that *perfectibility*, social virtues, and
> the other faculties which Natural man had received in
> potentiality could never develop by themselves, that in
> order to develop, they needed the chance combination
> of several foreign causes which might never have arisen

and without which he would have remained eternally in his primitive condition.[34]

Rousseau remains vague on the 'several foreign causes' that sealed off the state of nature and started denaturation. In society, simplicity became a social virtue after the accident that started history and saw the birth of organized communities. We know that social man has not preserved intact the simplicity of natural man; what we see here is simplicity as the marker of the accident that severed the man of man from the man of nature. Simplicity is not an original condition to be regained; simplicity as virtue is evidence that the accident happened. Living a simple life is embracing the possibility that things may change unexpectedly, that true virtue is not premeditated but heroic, because it is accidental. Social man is prepared, adapted, qualified, predisposed and rehearsed, always focusing on the future and preparing for it. The simple man is ready for everything because he is ready for nothing in particular.

Socrates was ready to die, that's what he learnt from philosophy. Christ was not ready to die: 'My God, my God, why have you forsaken me?' asked the simple man, son of God on the Cross, until he proclaimed his victorious, 'it is finished.'

While no one doubts the story of Socrates, no one should doubt the story of Christ, says the vicar, even if it is narrated in a text full of mysteries and contradictions which defy the subtlest capacity for reason. And what to do with such contradictions? Accept them. 'This is the involuntary scepticism in which I have remained,'[35] confesses the vicar, continuing:

But this scepticism is in no way painful for me, because it does not extend to the points essential to practice and because I am quite decided on the principles of all my duties. I serve God in the simplicity of my heart. I seek to know only what is important for my conduct.[36]

Involuntary scepticism is the union of the simplicity of the heart with the complications of reason, the involuntary acquiescence of truth to the incapacity of reason to deliberate and stand still. The simplicity of the heart curtails the flight of reason and aligns knowledge with necessity.

Rousseau extricated simplicity from discourses of oneness as origin or origin as oneness and from debates on ontology and primitivism. Civil simplicity is not atavistic, nor is it the sudden resurgence of ancestral traits lost for generations. Living simply, for perfectible beings engaged in history, means accepting the fact that accidents are opportunities for virtue to appear in its purest form. Being simple means welcoming the possibility of accidents and change. Simplicity is not the manifestation of the idea of simplicity; it is an openness to possibility, the possibility of possibilities.

Much of Rousseau's philosophical project was aimed at reawakening the sentiment of life through an awareness of being in the moment and being open to what emerges in that state. His conception of simplicity as the unobstructed access to living as it happens, and to life in general, prompted him to write this auto-biographical work. Henry David Thoreau would adopt a similar philosophy when he set out to document and live a simple life: 'Moreover, I, on my side, require of every writer, first or last, a simple and sincere account of his own life.'[37] First-hand experiences and first-hand accounts supply the basis of the Genevan and the American philosophers. Both philosophers have inspired generations to change their views on humankind and associations between people. More importantly, perhaps, both objected to the mechanization of men: 'he has no time to be any thing but a machine,' wrote Thoreau about his fellow men.[38] Modern man is busy being someone he is not just to respond to the demands of others. For Rousseau and Thoreau, simplicity can remedy the divisions within the self and even help a split self to coalesce. The reform they both worked towards was one of authenticity and integrity unhindered by excess, finery and divisions. 'Most of the luxuries, and many of the so-called comforts of life, are not only not indispensable, but positive hinderances to the elevation of mankind,' wrote Thoreau.[39] To elevate oneself and others one must observe and better understand oneself and others. The only way to achieve this is to commit to voluntary poverty: to renounce material riches to become spiritually richer is the responsibility of the simple philosopher living in the woods. He believed that

> To be a philosopher is not merely to have subtle thoughts,
> nor even found a school, but so to love wisdom as to live
> according to its dictates, a life of simplicity, independence,
> magnanimity, and trust. It is to solve some of the problems
> of life, not only theoretically, but practically.[40]

Here, the simple life is at the service of wisdom, and the greatest wisdom is to live differently, independently and charitably, but most of all to live 'deliberately', a word dear to adepts of simplicity like Thoreau and Rousseau. The philosopher living in simplicity aspires to 'maintain his vital heat by better methods than other men'.[41] His quest is life itself:

I went to the woods because I wished to live deliberately, to front only the essential facts of life, and see if I could not learn what it had to teach, and not, when I came to die, discover that I had not lived. I did not wish to live what was not life, living is so dear ... I wanted to live deep and suck out all the marrow of life, to live so sturdily and Spartan-like as to put to rout all that was not life . . . to drive life into a corner, and reduce it to its lowest terms.[42]

Whereas Rousseau, and Diogenes before him, looked for the man behind the screen of convention and denaturation, Thoreau looked for something greater still: life itself. He went on a hunt for life, wanting to catch it to discover whatever it was, good or bad, 'mean' or 'sublime', to use his terms. But to catch life one must live wisely and according to the dictates of established wisdom: '"Simplicity, simplicity, simplicity!" I say, let your affairs be as two or three, and not a hundred or a thousand.'[43] His method: 'Simplify, simplify. Instead of three meals a day, if it be necessary eat but one.'[44] To simplify is to reduce one's needs to what is absolutely necessary for subsistence while still living a life of independence, magnanimity and trust, the other three dictates of wisdom.

For over two years, starting on 4 July 1845, Thoreau lived in a cabin he built near Walden Pond in Massachusetts. The cabin was only a twenty-minute walk to Concord, the site of his family home, to which he would return regularly. Walden Pond was an attraction for bathers in the summer and skaters in the winter, with the visitors interrupting the eremitism of the pseudo-recluse. Does the fact of his proximity to others make his experience, and his account of it, which took him about nine years to write in seven manuscript versions, less valuable? No. But the apparent contradiction is an invitation to take it with a grain of salt, a condiment that he, incidentally, called the 'grossest of groceries', unnecessary to life.[45]

An observation of eating and buying habits motivated Thoreau to grow and make his own food instead of buying ready-made or imported products. The following excerpt from *Walden* has traversed history intact:

> Every New Englander might easily raise all his own bread-stuffs in this land of rye and Indian corn, and not depend on distant and fluctuating markets for them. Yet so far are we from simplicity and independence that, in Concord, fresh and sweet meal is rarely sold in the shops ... For the most part the farmer gives to his cattle and hogs the grain of his own producing, and buys flour, which is at least no more wholesome, at a greater cost, at the store. I saw that I could easily raise my bushel or two of rye and Indian corn ... I found by experiment that I could make a very good molasses either of pumpkins or beets, and I knew that I needed only to set out a few maples to obtain it more easily still, and while these were growing I could use various substitutes beside those which I have named, 'For,' as the Forefathers sang, –
>
> 'we can make liquor to sweeten our lips
> Of pumpkins and parsnips and walnut-tree chips.'[46]

Simplicity and independence, two objects of praise, follow from cultivating one's own crops, being economical in one's choices and consumption, observing one's immediate environment to decide what to grow, and listening to the wisdom preserved in old drinking songs. One word captures the folk wisdom: substitute. No simple living without substitution or profanation, to borrow Giorgio Agamben's idea. Profanation is the reclaiming of an object from a sacred or revered sphere to which it has been relegated by decree, whether religious, political or economic. The object is reclaimed from the sacred sphere to be restored to common use, shows Agamben. 'The capitalist religion', he writes, 'in its extreme phase aims at creating something absolutely unprofanable' whose alternative uses are never disclosed.[47] Making molasses or liquor out of pumpkins amounts to the type of profanation that makes simple living a political act of independence and resistance against the 'capitalist religion', a civil disobedience against the one-use-only law enforced by the High Priests of consumerism. The aim of simple living is not to restore things to their original and single use, if they ever had one; in living simply one takes advantage of the multiple uses of things to open up further possibilities. The spirit of invention and the spirit of profanation are complementary. With substitutes, Thoreau detached himself from money and the exchange of goods – 'I could avoid all trade and barter, so far as my food was concerned.'[48] New Englanders continued to feed hogs with grain they grew while buying high-priced flour at the store.

Thoreau's decision to live in the woods of Walden on the property of his mentor Ralph Waldo Emerson was prompted by a desire, perhaps a profound need, to write about his brother's death. Living simply was in a sense a laborious but salutary experience – pondering death while at the same time living fully from a little. That experience alone set him apart from his fellow

men. It should not come as a surprise that Thoreau was compared, much like Rousseau before him, with the philosopher
who lived in a *pithos*. 'A Yankee Diogenes' is the title of a review
written by the novelist and journalist Charles Briggs and published in October 1854. What made him a Diogenes was not an
endorsement of Cynicism as a philosophy; in fact, Briggs admits
that Thoreau was not a Cynic. But his decision to live in the margins of society made him one in the eyes of New Englanders,
whose 'character is essentially anti-Diogenic'.[49] New Englanders
were not fond of solitude because there was no money in seclu-
sion. Briggs remarks that Thoreau's aim was 'the very remarkable
one of trying to be something, while he lived upon nothing; in
opposition to the general rule of striving to live upon something,
while doing nothing'.[50]

In December 1854, a few months after the first publication of
Walden, or, Life in the Woods, Thoreau delivered a lecture called
'Life without Principle'.

> It is remarkable that there is little or nothing to be remem-
> bered written on the subject of getting a living: how to
> make getting a living not merely honest and honorable,
> but altogether inviting and glorious; for if *getting* a living
> is not so, then living is not.[51]

In his view, glory is a more enticing reward than mere virtue. The
direction of the gaze plays a part in achieving a glorious yet simple
life. Thoreau illustrates this point with a quote: 'Greatness doth
not approach him who is forever looking down; and all those
who are looking high are growing poor.'[52] In the same lecture, he
disclosed his contempt for activities that serve only individuals

at the expense of the greater good. Worse, societies governed by market economies, and driven by a race for innovation at all cost, denature men: 'Cold and hunger seem more friendly to my nature than those methods which men have adopted and advise to ward them off.'[53] Better to be cold and hungry than to sacrifice one's conscience to market forces and their arsenal of superfluous goods. Enterprise and progress have become, in some instances, the enemies of human nature, which can deal with natural assaults but is unequipped to win wars waged by men themselves. He stated: 'The ways in which most men get their living, that is, live, are mere makeshifts, and a shirking of the real business of life – chiefly because they do not know, but partly because they do not mean, any better.'[54]

Ignorance and avoidance are curses; knowledge, learning and experience are the true business of life. The business of life he calls 'wisdom'. 'The hog who gets his living by stirring up the soil so, would be ashamed' of the company of such unwise men.[55] But if nothing is done, if men continue to prefer ignorance over knowledge and idleness over action, if they continue to look down for fear of the poverty that comes with looking up, then the future looks bleak: 'The conclusion will be, that mankind will hang itself upon a tree.'[56] If there is a tree left; in Thoreau's time there were still woods to live in.

After a rather unremarkable debut, Thoreau could not predict that his account of life in the woods would inspire generation after generation. *Walden* was recently turned into a video game that has been received with great acclaim. Perhaps there is some tragic irony here that the praise for doing, learning and simple living should become a virtual game played on a machine while the player stares at a screen. Is this the ultimate simplicity, when physical obstacles have been lifted, when access to all possibilities is granted to the imagination? No, for to simplify is to be in immediate contact with the materiality of things and to retain the awareness of being in the moment while looking at the world – and up. Emerson, the *maître à penser* of Thoreau, knew that. 'The simplicity of the universe is very different from the simplicity of a machine,' he wrote in his 'Spiritual Laws'.[57] The simplicity of the universe cannot be easily read and is inexhaustible; the simplicity of a machine is finite and understandable. In an oft-quoted passage from 'Literary Ethics', a lecture delivered in July 1838, Emerson equates simplicity with greatness, a quality unavailable to machines at the time of writing and possibly still today. 'Nothing is more simple than greatness; indeed, to be simple is to be great.'[58] The great man or woman is not one who surrenders to private desires and impulses, and easily succumbs to the 'activity of the understanding', but the one who lets the universal speak through him or her, the one who is 'giving leave and amplest privilege to the spontaneous sentiment', the one willing to 'desert the tradition for a spontaneous thought'.[59] Emerson was not apologetic when he wrote about the greatness of man found in simple thoughts and unmediated vision. 'The superiority of the man is in the simplicity of his thought, that he has no obstruction, but looks straight at the pure fact, with no color of option.'[60] A simple mind 'lives now, and absorbs past and future into the present hour'.[61] The idea that the simple mind experiences the fullness of the present flows from Fénelon to Rousseau and finds perhaps its clearest expression in the English language in Emerson. For the last, simplicity is achromatic, the 'no color' of the previous quote:

Time and space are but physiological colors which the
eye makes, but the soul is light: where it is, is day; where
it was, is night . . . These roses under my window make
no reference to former roses or to better ones; they are
for what they are; they exist with God to-day. There is
no time to them. There is simply the rose; it is perfect in
every moment of its existence . . . He cannot be happy
and strong until he too lives with nature in the present,
above time.[62]

The simple mind can be like the simple rose if it surrenders to the
present and accepts the fact that 'life only avails, not the having
lived.'[63] Power, writes Emerson, is neither in the past nor in the
future but in the present, in the transition; it is energy, it is 'in the
shooting of the gulf.'[64] In nature, only what has power survives
changes, for 'nature suffers nothing to remain in her kingdoms
which cannot help itself.'[65] Accepting this simple fact of the
self-reliance of nature constitutes the basis for transcendentalist
ethics. As the world emanates from consciousness, it becomes
evident that 'it is simpler to be self-dependent.'[66]

Rousseau, Thoreau and Emerson were preoccupied with what
makes life simple rather than how to make a living. In the end,
their ethics value life above all; and the greatest manifestations
of life are to be found in nature. What simplicity uncovers, and
simple living attempts to perpetuate through deliberation and
concerted actions, is the 'shooting of the gulf', the energy of life.
All three philosophers were acutely aware of the social, political,
industrial and cultural changes occurring as they were writing.
That their interest in simplicity was prompted by the revolutions
they witnessed is most likely. For them, the new ways of living did

not honour the complexity of life; they reduced life and the living to a set of consumerist ambitions, automatic activities, divisive practices and self-splitting experiences.

The simple life as painted by the Transcendalists inspired intentional communities such as the Fruitlands farm, founded in June 1843 in Harvard, Massachusetts, and disbanded abruptly in December of the same year. Philosophical conflicts and mismanagement of farming resources led to the demise of the community.[67] For the Fruitlanders, a simple life away from the hustle and bustle of society was unthinkable without a diet that excluded all animal products. While this experiment failed, the creed based on dietary restriction and physical health was the foundational idea for a variety of nineteenth-century movements, especially in Germany. While these *Lebensreform* or 'life reform' movements, which spread throughout Germany and Switzerland in the late nineteenth century, were not all directly influenced by the Transcendalists or Rousseau, their dietary and health priorities echoed those of Rousseau and Thoreau.

The *Lebensreform* grew out of disenchantment; a loss of faith in the political system to execute social reforms placed the onus on the individual, who was seen as the engine of change par excellence. For Gustav Struve (1805–1870), a German radical democrat with revolutionary views who acknowledged Rousseau's influence on his life choices, 'self-control, moderation, simplicity in everything one does, in short inner freedom' paved the long road to social justice.[68] These values created a sense of class identity among those who adopted them. Although the communities greatly diverged in their political and social views, from anarcho-socialists to xenophobic groups, they all retained a set of core values:

Despite their philosophical differences, however, these undertakings all had much in common. Each sought to reestablish communitarian values in rural locations at a time of rapid social atomization, on the basis of a more natural and self-sufficient lifestyle that embraced organic farming, vegetarianism, naturism, and homeopathy. Each was anti-capitalist and anti-materialist in its rhetoric, stressed youth as a value in itself, and developed a calendar of celebratory rituals. Moreover, the problem of 'too many philosophers, insufficient potato-diggers' was common to all such communities, whether left or right.[69]

The disproportion between philosophers and potato-diggers is a reference to the New Community, founded in 1900, in Schlachtensee near Berlin, which allegedly failed because there were not enough doers to adequately feed the many thinkers.[70] Head-heavy, the community collapsed. But this movement survived in the *Reformhaus* or health-food stores that opened in the early 1900s. Catering to the needs of health-conscientious customers, such stores have grown in popularity in Germany and in many other parts of the world. These have become the storefront of simple living 'lite'; they are the retailers of good health for the individual, for society at large, and for the planet. They seem to cater to educated, white middle-class social reformers who value individual freedom and personal health.[71] In its least demanding form, simple living with its rallying cry 'less is more' has become an aspiration for the class-conscious and ethical customer. For our convenience, simple living is now sold in stores; there is no need to build a cabin or to philosophize about simplicity.

FIVE

SIMPLICITY MADE SIMPLE

'With the tremendous development of technology, a completely new poverty has descended on mankind. And the reverse side of this poverty is the oppressive wealth of ideas that has been spread among people.'[1] In 1933 Walter Benjamin argued that unchecked technological advances result in a certain poverty of experience. Even the proliferation of ideas, 'oppressive' as it may be, cannot fill the experiential vacuum. And 'our poverty of experience is not merely poverty on the personal level, but poverty of human experience in general.'[2] People are poor in experience, yet they do not seek to alleviate experiential poverty with new experiences. They compensate by consuming culture and news masquerading as culture. Ad nauseam compensation leads to satiation and fatigue. 'You are all so tired, just because you have failed to concentrate your thoughts on a simple but ambitious plan.'[3] In their fatigue, people transfer their 'simple but magnificent existence' on to dream-like figures using dissociating devices; as they do, they purge their own existence of simplicity and magnificence.[4] In the end, poverty of experience leads to existential poverty.

Benjamin believed a new and positive 'barbarism' may be the answer: 'For what does the poverty of experience do for the barbarian? It forces him to start from scratch; to make a new start; to make a little go a long way; to begin with a little and build up further, looking neither left nor right.'[5] Benjamin could be defining the simple life: a life rooted in experience, a life growing from the rich substrate of immediate experience, a life where economy of means and clarity of ends propel one forward – the simple life of a barbarian, forever a stranger in the land, always putting customs to the test of experience. All of Benjamin's barbarians share 'a total absence of illusion about the age and at the same time an unlimited commitment to it'.[6] Like them, advocates of simple living often exhibit a distrust of their age while they readily commit to local actions with long-term impact.

According to Walter Benjamin, it has become increasingly difficult to experience the world fully and at first hand. The walls and fences that divide up the land into tracts and units of private property hinder full experience. Likewise, the physical traces people leave on the world are reminders of their omnipresence. Benjamin is right; modern man and his progeny are busy leaving traces of themselves – whether graffiti, litter or initials – everywhere. The imprint of individual existences can be read on almost everything. The writing is on the world, so to speak. 'I have been here' – a sign that commemorates me and my presence in the world. The barbarian task is, then, to erase these traces, to remove the grids that demarcate all that is and to wipe off the world so as to start from a clean slate. Descartes, Newton and Einstein were such barbarians, writes Benjamin. Those were great minds. A barbarian who can wipe a slate clean to start anew displays all the traits of greatness. And for those who cannot wipe the slate clean? Can we partially erase the traces left on the world by amateur surveyors in need of posterity? If we must, can we leave identity markers without scarring the world?

To leave no trace on the slate is not a common wish, let alone a shared life goal. It takes a poet like Alexander Pope to show the simple plenitude of a life lived in the raw matter of experience without leaving the indelible markers of existence:

> Happy the man, whose wish and care
> A few paternal acres bound,
> Content to breathe his native air,
> > In his ground.
>
> Whose herds with milk, whose fields with bread,
> Whose flocks supply him with attire;
> Whose trees in summer yield him shade,
> > In winter fire.
>
> Bless'd who can unconcernedly find
> Hours, days, and years, slide soft away,
> In health of body, peace of mind,
> > Quiet by day.
>
> Sound sleep by night; study and ease,
> Together mix'd; sweet recreation;
> And innocence, which most does please,
> > With meditation.
>
> Thus let me live, unseen, unknown;
> Thus, unlamented let me die;
> Steal from the world, and not a stone
> > Tell where I lie.[7]

Pope was twelve when he wrote this ode. He and his family had just been forced to relocate to the countryside for religious reasons. The ode recalls Horace's *Epode* 2, 'beatus ille', which hails the joys of country life. Pope's 'Ode on Solitude' adds to the Latin poem the idea of stealing from the world, or leaving quietly, unseen, without an inscription on a tombstone. The simple man steals from the world without stealing anything from it. The simple life of the happy man in the ode ends without a word. He lived and left life behind him without a word to tell a story, with no writing on the wall of history to tell posterity, 'I was here.' A simple life is not prolonged in a string of words; it is lived in the moment.

In the age of instant communication concerning just about anything, an age when the word is written forever in the Cloud, the idea of stealing away from the world – unlamented, unseen, unknown – is becoming a frightening idea. We all leave carbon and digital footprints. The new technologies that prevent us from leaving this world unspoken and unsung represent so many ways to conquer, even in a seemingly evanescent manner, nothingness and death. Everybody writes in a virtual but permanent ink about experiences that are not fully theirs. New technologies turn machines into objects of pleasure. If we were not afraid of death, writes Henri Bergson, such pleasures would just vanish into thin air, taking with them the hot balloon machines that created them; they would be replaced by joy or simplicity of life, which would come from a 'diffused mystical intuition'.[8] In *Two Sources on Morality and Religion* (1932), Bergson wrote about the possibility of returning to a simpler, if not a simple, life. He asked whether artificial needs were generated by scientific progress, such as new technologies, or whether new technologies generated new needs.

For him, science has been at the service of the spirit of invention, which has animated men and women for centuries.[9] The spirit of invention from which science hails has changed the world and people's minds. In creating new needs, scientists, inventors and their many followers care little whether their inventions worked for the greater good or merely satisfied artificial desires and pleasures. People bear the responsibility for using machines and technologies to a moral end, and for simplifying rather than complicating their existence needlessly.[10]

The revolution in the way we use machines starts with the body. With every new technological and mechanical invention, even with the introduction of basic tools, man has created extensions of his own body to the point that his strength and size have grown immeasurably larger than his soul.[11] The shrivelled soul inhabits an extended body, which it no longer governs. The disproportion between soul and body explains the prioritization of artificial needs and the quest for immediate physical pleasures over long-term care. Here is the source of moral drift. For Bergson, machines and technologies should help us rise above the physical to reach beyond the world and look to the skies. Machines should assist the soul. Only the most complete and active mysticism, writes Bergson, served by human inventions, should regulate the operation of machines. This 'complete mysticism' is defined as the simplicity of a total experience, ideal and more than human, where the subjective and the objective become one as a total presence.[12]

In the philosophical project of Vladimir Jankélévitch, the simple life never acquires the suprahuman quality found in Bergson, his teacher. Jankélévitch puts forth two simplicities, one called simplicity *a qua*, the simplicity of origins, and simplicity *ad quam,* to which one returns by way of simplifications of life. Two ideas stand out in his essay on simplicity: one, simplicity is a decision or act directed by the intention to not itemize, fracture, dissect or sunder. The simple mind is not full of recesses, nooks and hiding places formed by a consciousness fearful of its own shadow. It is level and one. Moreover, only the simple inner self, which is undivided and whole, can find another one to love; as Jankélévitch put it, the self was waiting to be one inside in order to find outside a true 'other' to love, not just another image of itself. The divided self, in contrast, is in permanent and insistent dialogue with parts of itself, within and outside of itself – fictitious dialogues inside and projections of itself onto others. The simple self, on the contrary, has found a true and real other in the other.[13] Simplicity becomes the condition for true and wholesome relations, and love.

The other idea Jankélévitch develops in his essay is simplicity as improvisation. When consciousness is muted and one, it becomes available to the moment and to the possibilities of the present. The simple man is no *homo economicus*: he does not work for the future, does not have money in the bank, nor does he save for his retirement. He improvises: he surrenders to the fecundity of the present, to paraphrase Jankélévitch.[14] The plenitude of the present cannot be quantified, and certainly not monetized; what presents itself is welcomed without preparation or pomp, or it is received with an 'instantaneous preparation' as it emerges.[15] Simplicity is improvisation, simplicity is love. Jankélévitch's simplicity is about life with others in the abundance of the moment. It is also simplicity as action, not beatitude nor mysticism, and certainly not heroism, however humble it may be, as in Bergson's philosophy.

Today, notions of simple living and technology are enmeshed: simple mobile applications are coming to the rescue of a life that's become too complicated. There remain, however, areas of experience and existence where the encroachment of technology is less discernible and more insidious. Companies like Apple provide customers with weekly reports of mobile device use in a dubious attempt to encourage self-restraint. But resistance to technological imperiousness is mounting. Even in technophilic cultures, Neo-Luddite strongholds are not showing signs of surrender. 'Will 2018 be the year of the neo-luddite?' asked Jamie Bartlett in *The Guardian*.[16] The evidence against technology is stacking up, with allegations of Russian meddling in American elections, countless violations of online privacy and the increasing extent of the dark net. Democracy is under technological threat: 'In the coming few years either tech will destroy democracy and the social order as we know it, or politics will stamp its authority over the digital world. It is increasingly clear that technology is currently winning this battle, crushing a diminished and feeble opponent.'[17]

The battle is raging. In the last few years, low-tech lifestyles and off-grid living have been appealing to a growing number of people. New movements like 'slow-living', also called 'slow-tech', celebrate patience as a virtue. The reformed or moderate Luddism preached by Jamie Bartlett may appeal to those who shun the apocalyptic views of hardcore technophobes. But the movement is radicalizing under old banners.

Theodore Kaczynski, also known as the Unabomber, advocated for a new Luddism. His manifesto, entitled *Industrial Society and Its Future*, was published in 1995 after almost two decades of anti-technology activism and violent acts, including bombings resulting in three deaths and many serious injuries. The treatise identifies the many ills – such as loss of freedom and psychological violence – perpetrated by unbridled technological progress.

Kaczynski grounded his *Technological Slavery*, a collection of essays published in 2008, in four main ideas:

(1) Technological progress is carrying us to inevitable disaster; (2) Only the collapse of modern technological civilization can avert disaster; (3) The political left is technological society's first line of defense against revolution; (4) What is needed is a new revolutionary movement, dedicated to the elimination of technological society.[18]

In his introduction to the book, David Skrbina expanded on one of the *topoi* of Luddism: humans have not evolved to deal with technological advances of such magnitude as we see today. Our physical and psychological inability to cope with the current effects of technology and our intellectual incapacity to predict where such advances will take us should raise alarm bells. They do. But Skrbina hopes that technology is on course to its own destruction.[19] *Technological Slavery* includes a chapter that debunks the anarcho-primitivist myth of hunter-gatherer groups as models for today's societies. Ted Kaczynski opposes those he calls 'soft-headed dreamers, lazies, and charlatans', but he concedes that primitive people were not affected by chronic stress generated by technology, as we are; that primitive practices did not destroy the environment, as ours do; and above all, that members of primitive societies lived much freer lives than we do.[20] Freedom from technological tyranny is the prime mover of ideologies endorsed by Ted Kaczynski and his epigones.

Anti-technology groups bring to light some of the dangers of rampant technological expansion. The more radical among them promote liberation from technology through action, even the kind of action that jeopardizes deeply entrenched democratic values, as equality and peace. Wildism, an anti-civilization movement, is a case in point. Ethology and socio-biology provide its ideological armature. Partisans defend a return to indigenous ways of life even if such ways foster endemic violence. They have adopted a two-pronged strategy: one, 'rewilding' what has been wrongfully extracted from nature and two, listening to the call of the wild will in us. Progressivism, especially social progressivism, is the bête noire of the Wildists, who believe that any progress – understood as an unnatural modification of nature – leads to denaturation. Humanism as a commanding ideology and some of its modern offshoots like democracy and liberation movements are deemed unnatural. The profound fracture between Wildist views and political anarchism appears to be beyond repair, but the dialogue between some eco-anarchists and eco-socialists could be rekindled.

Samuel Alexander of the Simplicity Institute has put forward the concept of 'Wild Democracy'. For Alexander, stateless eco-anarchism, with its focus on education, resistance and renewal, is not antagonistic to the legislation-driven objectives of eco-socialists.[21] Rather than a sudden toppling of government, he argues for an ongoing revolution, championing environmental values and social justice. Such a revolution would curtail the rapid expansion of unregulated capitalism.[22] Wild Democracy happens in a political and cultural space where imaginations have been rewilded:

This opening or rewilding of the imagination is not an insignificant precondition of transformative change. There will be no deliberate transition beyond capitalism – whether eco-socialist, eco-anarchist, or another other way – until more people see that other worlds are possible. In that light, all visions of alternative modes of living should be encouraged in order to help ignite people's revolutionary imaginations . . . The real problem, I contend, is figuring out how to open up people's imaginations to the *very possibility* of alternative modes of existence.[23]

Alexander is right. The rewilding of the imagination to the possibility of simpler lives lived in the moment while preparing for the future is probably as critical and vital as it is difficult to achieve. His argument is valid and timely. His idea of rewilding imaginations taps an earlier source with considerable cultural appeal. Alexander's 'Wild Democracy' report closes with a quote from Thoreau's *A Week on the Concord and Merrimack Rivers*: 'This world is but a canvas to the imagination.'[24] The exact words of Thoreau read: 'This world is but a canvas to our imaginations.'[25] Alexander's emendation of the possessive adjective and the plural form in the original text is significant. If by 'our imaginations' Thoreau meant our creative imagination, then the world spreads before us like a blank slate onto which we project images. The Romantic idea of an active and creative imagination still prevails; it paints the world with broad strokes as it takes possession of it with every brush. Could our imaginations instead dispossess us of the world?

According to Martin Heidegger, 'Technology is a mode of revealing.'[26] What is revealed in technology is the world as 'standing reserve'. 'The revealing that rules in modern technology is a "challenging" [*Herausfordern*], which puts to nature the unreasonable demand that it supply energy that can be extracted and stored as such,' writes Heidegger in his essay, 'The Question concerning

Technology.'[27] In a technological world, the great depths of the earth, a field, a river are all 'challenged' to deliver energies, which in turn are 'challenged-forth' to produce heat; heat is 'challenged-forth' to produce steam, steam is 'challenged-forth' to activate an engine, which carries coal, and so on. The challenging-forth never ends nor is it indeterminate. The revealing reveals itself to itself as it regulates and secures its complex network of paths. 'Everywhere everything is ordered to stand by, to be immediately at hand, indeed to stand there just so that it may be on call for a further ordering. Whatever is ordered about in this way has its own standing. We call it standing-reserve [*Bestand*].'[28]

Everything is challenged, ordered and interchanged in this 'standing-reserve' we call real.[29] Man is certainly included in the 'standing-reserve', often under the category 'human resources', although he retains some power to give direction to the ordering.[30] Likewise, Nature has retained some power in her capacity to produce raw material; she can still reveal herself independently of man or technology.

Everything that is challenged or called forth is ordered and assembled in the active process of 'Enframing' [*Ge-stell*]. Enframing can overpower any other forms of revealing. It conceals man from man: '*nowhere does man today any longer encounter himself, i.e., his essence.*'[31] Enframing can conceal how the world reveals itself, and even conceal the revealing of itself:

> The threat to man does not come in the first instance from the potentially lethal machines and apparatus of technology. The actual threat has already affected man in his essence. The rule of Enframing threatens man with the possibility that it could be denied to him to enter into a

more original revealing and hence to experience the call of a more primal truth.[32]

Enframing and the process that views the world as a 'standing-reserve' determine humanity's relationship to the world. Enframing conceals other forms of revealing, as stated in the above excerpt, limiting our capacities to hear a wilder or more 'primal truth'. But in Enframing, Heidegger explains, lies the possibility of caring for the world, not destroying it. The Greek word *technē*, writes Heidegger, conveys the ideas of instrumentality and the arts, or *poiesis*. *Poiesis* is the bringing-forth into existence achieved by the poet and the artisan. Heidegger's essay invites the reader to see the world not only as a 'standing-reserve' but as *poiesis*, as a participation in the process of coming into being, of revealing. For the poet, the world reveals itself as it is: 'The poetical brings the true into the splendour of . . . that which shines forth most purely. The poetical thoroughly pervades every art, every revealing of coming to presence into the beautiful.'[33] That which shines forth most purely is the truth. That particular revealing needs to be protected from the expansion of Enframing; it is art that may help us question technology.

Heidegger's ideas open up novel ways of thinking about a simple life. Art and Enframing are different types of revealing, but all revealing comes with its corollary opposite: concealing. The tension between the two arises in works of art and in craftsmanship. The example of the cabinetmaker's apprentice illustrates the point:

His learning is not mere practice, to gain facility in the use of tools. Nor does he merely gather knowledge about the customary forms of the things he is to build. If he is to become a true cabinetmaker, he makes himself answer and respond above all to the different kinds of wood and to the shapes slumbering within wood – to wood as it enters into man's dwelling with all the hidden riches of its nature. In fact, this relatedness to wood is what maintains the whole craft. Without that relatedness, the craft will never be anything but empty busywork, any occupation with it will be determined exclusively by business concerns. Every handicraft, all human dealings are constantly in that danger.[34]

The nature of the cabinetmaker's relatedness to the raw material makes the difference between craft and industry. Moreover, the cabinetmaker first 'makes himself'. He works on himself first to be able and to will to 'answer and respond' to the quality of the wood. That initial work on himself completed, he can 'answer and respond' to what is revealed as he works; in his work, he learns that there is no revealing without concealing. The relatedness to the raw material translates as attention both to what things are and to how we respond to them. The relatedness also preserves the secrets or 'hidden riches' of raw material instead of ordering it. Ultimately, the relatedness can be understood as the simultaneous presence of the craftsman, the wood and the object being revealed. But accepting the once hidden, now revealed, riches of the world without trying to order them requires effort and humility, two virtues present in a simple life.

The idea of the world revealing and concealing not something other than itself, but itself as one, underlies simple living in many respects. Clément Rosset dedicated much of his philosophical career to probing mental attitudes towards the real. He defines the real as 'the sum of the events that are called into existence'.[35] And Rosset sees in simplicity 'the coincidence of the real with itself', which, he concedes, is a rare occurrence.[36] Perceiving the coincidence of the real with the real requires courage or idiocy, possibly both. He suggests:

> There is nothing more fragile than the human faculty for consenting to reality, for accepting unreservedly the imperious prerogative of the real. That faculty is so often found wanting that it seems reasonable to imagine it does involve the recognition of an inalienable right – the right of the real to be perceived – but represents a kind of conditional, provisional *tolerance*. A tolerance anyone can suspend at will, as soon as the circumstances demand it . . .[37]

Our threshold of tolerance for the real is constantly being tested by nothing else than the real itself. Increasingly the real provokes in us adverse reactions such as frustration, disgust and anger, so that our tolerance for it shows clear signs of erosion. On the contrary, we seem to tolerate with greater ease – we even welcome – a variety of expedients, such as virtual reality, which steer reality away from us. If applications of virtual reality have developed rather recently, complications, distractions and escapisms of all sorts are not new phenomena. Complicating – etymologically, folding together or layering instead of unfolding or simplifying – proves a sure way of vetoing the real. Rosset juxtaposes what he calls the 'distaste for the simple' with the taste for complication:

> At a first level, distaste for the simple merely expresses a taste for complication: the complicated manoeuvre is

preferred to the simple attitude, even if the goal pursued in each case is the same – and even if this excess of complication may mean missing that goal. At a second level, however, which does not eliminate the first but deepens and elucidates it, distaste for the simple denotes fear in the face of the unique, distance from *the thing itself*, the taste for *complication* expressing in the first instance a need for *duplication* required for the evasive acceptance of a real whose raw uniqueness is instinctively sensed to be indigestible. Understood in this way, this rejection of the simple enables us to understand why the affected engage in their affection – not so much to seem clever to others as to subdue the lustre of the real, the vividness of which wounds them with its intolerable uniqueness. Things are bearable only if mediated, doubled: there is nothing in this world that can be taken 'just as it is'.[38]

The goal to reach may be clear and the steps to reach it simple, but I vote for the complicated course. I see the simpler way to my destination and choose not to follow it. The detours and meanders do not negate the existence of the straight route, but it is my choice to see the straight route and decide to walk ramblingly, even to exhaustion, to my destination. Often the longer way appears the freer way: the path I have chosen. But as I walk on the long and tortuous road I never quite lose sight of the short way: annoyingly, it remains within sight, it pops up unpredictably. In *The Real and Its Double*, Rosset describes this acceptance– rejection of the real as more common than Freudian *repression* or Lacanian *foreclosure*.

This other way of being rid of the real resembles a correct line of reasoning that ends in an aberrant conclusion. It is an accurate perception that turns out to be incapable of issuing in behaviour adapted to that perception. In this case I do not refuse to see, nor do I in any way deny the real that is shown to me. But my consent stops there. I have seen something and accepted it but don't ask more of me than that. In all other ways, I maintain my previous point of view, persist in my earlier behaviour, as though I had seen nothing. Paradoxically, my present perception and my earlier standpoint coexist. What we have here is a perception that is not so much erroneous as *useless*.[39]

The useless perception of the real is not ignored but displaced. It is not a case of blindness but a severe case of *seeing double*.[40] As Rosset argues, the double is both itself and other at once, neither acceptance nor rejection of the other. The real, or 'the sum of events called into existence', is perceived as ineluctable and unmodifiable, but capable of being doubled. It is ineluctable because the event that comes into existence does so in a unique way, excluding other ways of coming into existence. What is perceived in the perception of the coming into existence of an event is the uniqueness of its realization.[41] We see the real as unique or simple. We also see the real as unmodifiable. Because it is constantly changing it is formless; what is formless cannot be reformed or modified.[42] The real is constitutionally ever changing, unmodifiable and simple. Yet accepting such a definition of the real is not for everyone.

The real is bearable only when it is mediated or complicated. We complicate the real, animated as we are by intellectual curiosity and a desire to pierce the secrets of the real. When we complicate it, we supplement the real with meanings that it did not possess; we find in it secrets which we believe it is jealously guarding. But the real has no secrets because it has nothing to hide.[43] It is easier to believe that the real is keeping something from us than tolerating its simplicity. But if one remains open to the simplicity of the real, one must accept the double risk of triumph and humiliation – triumph in being unique, in being the only one to see things for what they are; humiliation at being alone, just one, almost no one, and in the end, perhaps being no one with this experience.[44] When we experience even fleetingly the simplicity of the real, don't we feel triumph in the experience and humiliation at the ease with which it was experienced? My experience of the real is triumphantly and humiliatingly simple. A life lived simply is a life ready to embrace the humiliation, humility and the triumph of the real seen 'just as it is', of the world experienced 'just as it is'.

Experiencing the world as real presents challenges; searching for the simplicity and reality of the self requires concessions and further humility on the part of the querent. The personal self – the one onto which we latch the idea of identity – is best described in an anecdote reported by Clément Rosset. After the death of his father, a local printer, his son decided to take over the shop. Going through the printing stock, he happened upon a fat envelope labelled with the words 'do not open'. For six years he resisted the temptation to open it; finally, he gave in. What did he find in the envelope labelled 'do not open'? Over one hundred 'do not open' labels.[45] Personal identity is like this envelope, full of messages of inconsequential significance.[46] This story frames Rosset's definitions of personal and social identities. Personal identity is in fact a borrowed identity acquired through continuous imitations of others. In turn, the imitated self is made up of imitations of other selves. The chains of borrowed or copied identities is what Rosset calls social identities.[47] The self is constituted by others, themselves constituted by others.

In another example, Rosset invokes Lacan, who showed that the identity of a married man, for instance, is not predicated on the verifiable fact that he is a husband, but rather that someone else is his wife.[48] Removed from the company of someone else, here the wife, the solitary self experiences a loss of identity. What is acutely felt as a loss of identity is in fact the loss of the social self, which is imitated, never owned nor finite, according to Rosset. In this line of thought, to understand oneself one must only investigate the manifestations of our social selves. Introspection or the idea of finding an illusory core personal identity only leads to the disclosure of social identities acquired over myriad imitations of others. Together these imitations create a sense, illusory though it may be, of a coalesced and continuous self.[49] The idea of finding one's self as one and simple is ill-fated, according to Rosset. But the idea of being made from others and with others might revitalize a damaged sense of common good and justice.

Unlike the real, unique, unmodifiable, unpredictable and simple, the self is composite, constructed, modifiable and ordinary. These qualities of the self may be as intolerable to us as the unicity and simplicity of the real, which we try to modify by endless complications. We try to simplify the self to give it the unity that we refuse to the real. We complicate the simple and simplify the complex. Living a simple life may necessitate the distressing reversal of a set of values that many hold true; it may necessitate the questioning of principles inculcated from an early age. The self is not simple, one, but complex and never unique; the world is not complex but simple. This may form the basis of an ethics of care tending to that which is simple – unique, unmodifiable, irreplaceable. In this thought experiment, the simple and irreplaceable world needs our care because it is simple.

Most readers of this book will be familiar with the movement called Voluntary Simplicity. The term is generally attributed to Richard Gregg, a Quaker and advocate of Gandhi's ideas, who defined it in a pamphlet, *The Value of Voluntary Simplicity*, published in 1936. Voluntary Simplicity, Gregg stated, is the expression of 'singleness of purpose, sincerity and honesty within, as well as avoidance of exterior clutter, of many possessions irrelevant to the chief purpose of life'.[50] The singleness of purpose and the chief purpose of life are life itself: mine, other people's and the world's. Over the years, Voluntary Simplicity has grown and mingled with other movements of a similar kind and with complementary ambitions. Duane Elgin's *Voluntary Simplicity: Toward a Way of Life That Is Outwardly Simple, Inwardly Rich*, originally published in 1981, brought under one cover many of the guiding principles of a social and cultural movement which had been embracing values originating in 1960s' and 1970s' counter-cultures. Civil rights, the women's liberation and gay rights movements, concern for the environment and anti-consumerism all fed into the Voluntary Simplicity movement. Elgin's book was followed by a series of works extolling the virtues of the simple life, such as Sarah Ban Breathnach's *Simple Abundance* (1995), which sold millions of copies, becoming one of the best-sellers of the 1990s, and Cecile Andrew's *The Circle of Simplicity: Return to the Good Life* (1997), which gave a new impetus to the movement. Voluntary

Simplicity, composed of a set of broad values ranging from environmentalism, anti-consumerism and a search for the good life, is a movement so varied that no definition will do justice to the range of motivations that inspire participants and groups all over the world. Nevertheless, a new sense of urgency to save the planet mobilizes all voluntary simplifiers.

Who are the simplifiers? Samuel Alexander and Simon Ussher, co-directors of the Simplicity Institute, based in Australia, conducted a multinational survey of over 2,000 people in 2012 to better understand the motivations and habits of simplifiers.[51] Some of their findings are worth reproducing here. The first significant fact has to do with demographics: only 21 per cent of the participants lived in rural areas.[52] This confirms that the movement does not reflect some resurgence of primitivist impulses pushing people en masse to the countryside. This figure also means that the chances that the movement will expand to a larger segment of the global urban population are greater than anticipated. If it had only appealed to people in rural areas, its expansion would have been inhibited. Another notable fact gleaned from the responses to the survey is that 67 per cent of participants had voluntarily reduced their income. This number verifies, as the authors observe, that choosing simplicity involves a change in lifestyle associated with a reduction in income and consumption.[53] Next, 38 per cent of people changed jobs or careers and 48 per cent cut their working hours. In many cases, the decision to live a simpler life led to a relocation.[54] While for many simple living meant reducing expenditures, it also encouraged smarter buying choices and strategies prioritizing local and ecologically friendly products. Simplifiers acknowledged that decluttering is a significant part of a simpler lifestyle. However, how one views one's possessions means more than the tally of things owned. They mention the pleasure gained in recycling or upcycling. Food production is part of the simple life, with 83 per cent of participants growing some of their food, and 36 per cent of people report bartering or preferring other types of non-monetary exchanges. Only 13 per cent were vegetarian and a mere 4 per cent vegan, debunking another myth about simplifiers' dietary habits.[55] The survey also revealed that 67 per cent of simplifiers took part in community organization, while 52 per cent stated that spirituality is a part of their life. Significantly, 80 per cent thought that advanced technology is not antithetical to the simple life, although television, for one, does not appear to be the main source of leisure for simplifiers.[56]

Motivations to live a simpler life are as varied as simplifiers themselves. The environment, health, self-reliance, time for oneself or one's family, spirituality and social justice rank among the top reasons for adopting a simpler life.[57] The vast majority of people surveyed reported that they lived happier lives after they transitioned to a simpler lifestyle.[58] The decision to commit to simplicity long term led to adjustments in work and housing arrangements, as seen above. Some of the obstacles to simple living were related to work and housing. To live simply requires a reallocation of time from other activities and work. Commuting to work consumes much of people's time; an increase in travel time on relocating to a more affordable but more remote area steered people away from simple living.[59] Alexander and Ussher offer suggestions for social and political reforms that would encourage new simplifiers to join the movement: a shorter work week and relaxed work reduction regulations, for instance. Their findings offer, they hope, guidance for policymakers who are inclined to promote simple living. In the long term, perhaps, governments could devise a 'politics of simple living'.[60]

The survey reveals another significant hurdle to simple living: the ability to resist consumer temptation. Finding time in a busy schedule is the reason many shun simpler lives; the underlying reason to work more is, in many cases, motivated by the desire to buy more or upgrade. That temptations block the path to simplicity is a fact as old as the world, and this book has told of a few attempts to tame or eradicate worldly desires through ascetic practices. Today, such practices are deemed obsolete, ethically and politically questionable, or just radical. Their appeal to the great many is nil.

Resisting consumer temptations has become an even greater challenge than it ever was. The availability of inexpensive goods corrodes resistance to impulse buying; substances like sugar and fat, found in large amounts in readily available, cheap foods, create addictions. Peer pressure to have more and even more is one of the great drivers of capitalist economies. The idea that one's moral value is determined by one's possessions – 'I am only as good as what I own' – is rampant. These challenges are not exactly new, and in many ways, they are the reasons why some chose to simplify their lives in previous centuries. But today, goods, foods, external signs of riches and all manner of superfluous products are advertised, packaged and made available in such a way as to satisfy consumers' simplicity, we are told by marketers. 'To Keep Your Customers, Keep It Simple' is the title of an article published in the *Harvard Business Review* in 2012.[61] Since consumer loyalty has nosedived, targeted messaging has become the ultimate weapon to retain customers. The goal is not to make them happy, but to make them 'sticky'. Stickiness is defined as success in convincing customers to purchase, to repeat purchases and to spread the good word about a product. What makes customers stick? Simplicity.[62] Customers want to trust the information they are given on the product and be able to make a swift, yet informed, purchase decision from among a variety of goods. 'What consumers want from marketers is, simply, simplicity' is one of the mantras of marketing professionals.[63] Customers should be able to navigate and understand the product information with ease. Clear information should prompt customers to make a simple purchasing decision. The more information, the more convoluted the message, the more complex the decision process, the less likely one is to buy a product, marketing research has shown.

The marching orders for marketeers: have customers navigate, trust, decide, buy and repeat, all in record time. The more complex the products, the simpler the steps to 'stickiness' should be. The higher the 'decision simplicity index', the better for the product.[64] Simplicity boosts market economies. To make the purchase decision as simple as possible – how many products have the word 'simple' in their names? Tesco, one of the largest retailers in the world, sells a line of skincare products called 'Simple'. Products in this line are unscented, contain no harsh chemicals and are gentle; in other words, they are simple. Marks & Spencer has named its local shops 'Simply Food'. They sell food, not necessarily simple foods, and not just food either. The American magazine *Real Simple* has close to eight million readers. *Real Simple*, which is really neither, boasts enticing displays of foods, health products, household goods and general well-being enhancers. It is shopping made simple. Simplicity sells.

Examples of products featuring the word 'simple' are numerous. One merits special attention: Apple. Ken Segall, the author of *Insanely Simple* and *Think Simple*, was the mastermind behind the 'Think different' campaign that propelled Apple to the top. He is also accredited for adding the 'i-' to the Mac and for creating the durable legacy of the 'i-', a minuscule with a big history. The epigraph of *Insanely Simple* is a stroke of genius:

'Simplify, simplify.'
– Henry David Thoreau
'Simplify.'
– Apple

Segall had beaten the icon of American simplicity at his own game. Could anything be simpler in the American cultural landscape than a hut near a pond? Yes, a computer, the epitome of technological complexity for laypeople. He had even simplified Thoreau's formula by removing a superfluous 'simplify' from the motto. The name of the famous author of the first quotation even seems excessively long compared to the nicely concise 'Apple', fruit of the earth.

'Every one of Apple's revolutions was born of the company's devotion to Simplicity,' writes Segall.[65] Simplicity, which, judging from Segall's choice of words, acquired the status of a religion in the company, revolutionized the way we live our lives. Apple's greatest asset: adaptability: 'As the world changes, as technology changes, as the company itself adapts to change, the religion of Simplicity is the one constant. It's the set of values that allows Apple to turn technology into devices that are just too hard to resist.'[66]

It is this type of simplicity that makes it hard for us to adopt a simpler lifestyle, according to the list of challenges encountered by simplifiers. Apple's simplicity is everywhere, from slogans – the old iMac was 'simply amazing, and amazingly simple' – to product design, company structure and customer relations. Segall is quick to say that simplicity is hard work; thankfully, the benefits one reaps are worth the effort: 'By embracing the values of Simplicity, you will be the one who promotes change, keeps colleagues on course, and proves your value to the company day by day.'[67] This is an example of corporate simplicity at its best: engineering technological and social changes outside the company in the name of simplicity, and reining in colleagues and courting company managers, also in the name of simplicity. The 'religion of Simplicity' leads to statements like 'Simplicity is power, whether it's used by individuals or organizations.'[68] The God Simplicity, prime mover of the Apple revolution, remains finally rather elusive. We are never really told the nature of Simplicity and its attributes are unspoken; yet its divine omnipresence reigns uncontested like a *deus absconditus* that must be reckoned with. As a creator of all things, Simplicity is present in all things it creates:

> People of all ages, religions, cultures, and political beliefs prefer Simplicity. In fact, it's not just human beings who prefer it. This preference is burned into the basic wiring of all living cells. When it comes to ordinary, everyday decisions, most life-forms agree: The simpler path is the far more attractive one.
>
> Whether you're a person, dog, fish, or amoeba, you will respond more positively to the simpler solution – even if it isn't a conscious response. Businesspeople who understand, embrace, and leverage this fact are destined to achieve greater success than those who do not.[69]

This conception of simplicity is not unique to Segall and the Apple adventure. But his mixed metaphors are revealing of the larger, business-led views that are shaping our lives, and in many ways, our thoughts and ideas. First, on the metaphors: simplicity is 'burned', as one would burn a disk, into the 'wiring' of cells. It would be difficult to think of a more mechanistic view of life. At the same time, all life-forms, from you to the amoebas, are graced with decision-making powers and the capacity to agree or disagree (preferably not the latter) with the simpler solutions Apple offers to complex problems. That's the secret to success and the good life. Such statements amount to a series of oversimplifications that justify absolutist statements of this kind: 'The undeniable truth [is that] . . . people prefer simplicity.'[70] This 'built-in preference' leads to a conception of the world, the business world to be sure, that is binary – good simplicity vs bad complexity: 'While there exists this wonderful idea called Simplicity, there also exists that dark cloud called Complexity. Complexity can be powerful and seductive, so it should never be underestimated.'[71]

One would think that Segall is overstating the point for rhetorical purposes, and carefully choosing his religious metaphors for the same reason, but the world he is creating, his world, is not governed by simplicity, as he seems to think, but rather by simplism – oversimplifications and false equivalencies.

In the world of Apple, simplicity is preferred because we all have it, Segall believes, even if we don't know it; it is a world where the simple and righteous shall prevail, where they will 'defang', his word, the mighty enemy named Complex;[72] it is a world where simplicity turns into simplism, disguised as the 'love child' of 'Brains and Common Sense', which are capitalized in the text.[73] Simplism may parade as rational thinking, but it remains an intentional error of judgement with the intent to bend decisions in favour of the person professing the so-called simple truths. We choose simplicity, Segall says, because we are wired to do so; we can't resist it. This is an interesting philosophical question about free will, to be sure, but hardly one whose outcome is the good life. For Segall, Apple is here to simplify our lives because we really want our lives to be simple. In other words, Apple products, which are all products with a high Simplicity Index, make our decisions simpler to the point that they make decisions for us without us knowing it.

What do we have to lose in the oversimplification of our lives? Quite a lot. Save for a few who are getting much, very much indeed, out of simplicity; these are the architects of simplistic thinking:

> My style of deal-making is quite simple and straightforward. I aim very high, and then I just keep pushing and pushing and pushing to get what I'm after . . .
>
> To me it's very simple: if you're going to be thinking anyway, you might as well think big . . . One of the keys to thinking big is total focus. I think of it almost as a controlled neurosis, which is a quality I've noticed in many highly successful entrepreneurs. They're obsessive, they're driven, they're single-minded and sometimes they're almost maniacal, but it's all channeled into their work . . .
>
> I don't say this trait leads to a happy life, or a better life, but it's great when it comes to getting what you want.[74]

In Donald Trump's *The Art of the Deal*, simple thinking – defined as hyperbolic thinking and neurotic single-mindedness – is entirely at the service of greed, self-aggrandizement and self-exceptionalism. Unsupported claims abound, like the simplicity of big thinking being the natural gift of the very few. Some are born great . . . full stop. The advice contained in this largely autobiographical book on how to become a millionaire is hardly original. Yet the book cracks open a window on to the current and perilous simplism that has infected politics. Simplism is a two-step process: first, create confusion and chaos; then, offer simplistic solutions that work to your advantage.

Nobel Prize-winner Daniel Kahneman has demonstrated that when we are faced with a complex question, we often replace it with an easier one. In most instances, we are not aware of the substitution.[75] The answer given to the simplified question originates in anchored knowledge. Anchored knowledge, unreflective and limited in scope, is a reservoir of established personal truths. Tapping this source may help us avoid undue stress on cognitive processes, but it generally leads to cognitive bias. In response to the simpler question, simple if not simplistic answers will be preferred. Kahneman's research shows that other cognitive shortcuts are particularly plentiful in divisive political rhetoric. Experiments based on syllogisms have revealed that people who believe in a prefabricated conclusion will accept any arguments that lead to it even if those arguments prove illogical and flawed.[76] If the argument is founded on partial information, no further information will be sought; instead, conclusions will be reached faster.[77] Simplism flourishes in the fertile environments of cognitive biases and fallacies. In its extremist expression and bellicose manifestations, simplism is the enemy of simplicity as a way of life, which it deems unrealistic, retrograde and a violation of personal freedom. It often borrows ready-made arguments from the rhetoric of the Red Scare.

Research conducted by psychologist Jacob Feldman has shown that the simpler the argument, or the simpler the story, the less likely it is to be deemed accidental; it appears created or manufactured.[78] Too simple to be true. But structures that are simpler than expected are more likely to pique interest.[79] The Simplicity Theory, developed by Jean-Louis Dessalles, postulates that people are 'sensitive to *complexity drops*: i.e., to situations that are *simpler to describe than to explain*'.[80] An example of a complexity drop and its attending unexpectedness would be the following lottery draw: 1–2–3–4–5–6. This consecutive draw is simpler because a small amount of information suffices to describe it. A more expected draw with six random numbers would not garner the same interest and would require a more complex description.[81] In the end, a simpler draw will be less expected but more interesting. Perhaps draws that are both simple and interesting should raise concerns about tampering and possibly fraud. In other words, anything that lends itself to a simple description is not necessarily trustworthy, however appealing and cognitively satisfying that description or argument may be. Those who choose to live a simple life tend to approach 1–2–3–4–5–6 situations with a degree of measured caution. Resisting the temptation of whatever seems too simple at first sight is one of the first steps towards simple living.

Shunning substitutions and oversimplifications constitute a large part of simple living. Resisting simplism is not the easiest part of a simple life, as we are continually bombarded with reductionist ideas disguised as simple and sound reasoning, luring us into blind consumerism and fearful protectionism. Voluntary simplifiers are not individualistic, primitivist escapists, as they are sometimes painted; neither are they idealists detached from the realities of Western economic life. On the contrary, many are urbanites who have adopted a lifestyle governed by the ethical principles of benevolence and concern for others and the planet. Despite its expansion as a movement, simple living lags behind 'greener' lifestyles heralded by the mainstream media. As a way of life, it offers a range of solutions to the environmental ruin of our times, unchecked economic growth, rampant poverty and the growing unease with the current political situation. It is no redder than it is green, nor is it a 'Third Way'.

The Simplicity Movement is still an 'unmobilized constituency', as shown in the responses provided to Alexander and Ussher's survey.[82] Its lack of visibility on the Western political stage may stem from the low-level radicalization of the participants. Adopting a simpler lifestyle is not that difficult. Perhaps the ease with which one becomes a simplifier undermines the decision process that led to the simple action. There are degrees of commitment and these have been described at length; but, truth be told, a simpler life starts with a simple decision to act. The radicalization of that decision may be necessary for the movement to be noticed and to grow. Downshifters, as portrayed in Amitai Etzioni's typology of simplifiers, may not be aware that they are politically active.[83] They may not have the stamina of the '68 Generation activists, but the sum total of their decisions and actions add up in a global effort to save the planet. The choice to not buy superfluous products is not a sign of poor socialization; it is a political act of resistance, of economic disobedience committed while walking the aisle of the supermarket. Simple living is also joining an intentional community of shared and coherent values, but it is not just that. Typology does not help when it comes to understanding people's motivations: are they 'conscientious simplifiers' or 'precautious frugals'?[84] These types are primarily sketched to fine-tune marketing campaigns:

> In Germany, voluntary simplicity represents a remarkable segment (14.4%) and simultaneously an interesting target group for both green products as well as products that meet the need for lower consumption (e.g., durable products, sharing products). Thus, moderate simplifiers are moving away from the consumerist mainstream towards a more sustainable model of consumption. From a business perspective, moderate simplifiers are an interesting group for companies that are able to transmit the philosophy of a simple life through their products and services.[85]

The number of studies profiling voluntary simplifiers would baffle anyone unfamiliar with this growing research field and market. Businesses and marketers are hard at work roping simplifiers in. They even work hard to 'transmit the philosophy of a simple life' in their products, lines and advertisements. The fact of the matter is that there is no such thing as a monolithic, consensual and doctrinarian philosophy of simple living. But there may be an emerging philosophy of simple living grounded in the distrust of simplicity made simple.

CONCLUSION:
A SIMPLE VOICE

Speaking as someone who hates throwing away things without finding another use for them or mending them, I could not be more delighted if, at last, there is a growing awareness of the urgent need to get away from the throwaway society and to move towards a more circular economy.

PRINCE CHARLES[1]

It may be a sign that the times are changing when a multimillionaire and heir to the throne of the United Kingdom proclaims himself to be a champion of frugality. Of course, it may be easier for the rich to be frugal, but Prince Charles's actions testify to his genuine concern for the future of the planet. His official website boasts of the many environmental causes His Royal Highness has endorsed in the UK and abroad.[2] For the past forty years, he has been promoting economically viable projects with social and environmental benefits. However, like many people of lesser means who share his concerns about the environment, Prince Charles still operates within the framework of classical economics. In many ways, the solutions he publicly validates perpetuate the model that gave rise to the environmental crisis in the first place. However beneficial sustainable actions and policies may be, most of them are still driven by the principles of economic growth and development. Even domestic frugality, represented by the Prince as a 'circular economy', is governed by the same idea of unidirectional growth, pointing forward. Sustainability and intentional but selective frugality are concerned with steering the economy, global and domestic, in the right ethical direction. Most people would frown upon the idea of stalling or reversing economic growth, and Prince Charles's environmental positions are not entirely different from those adopted by many Green economists. Repurposing, zero-waste and natural resource efficiency are all bolstered by a faith in neoliberalism and the conviction that market economies – like life – self-preserve, self-heal and self-propagate. The general idea is that with new environmental economic incentives and a smarter propagation of sustainable priorities and actions, the current system will mend itself. Frugality and sustainability, the *mots du jour*, capture the now common theme that unbridled consumerism is bad for humanity and for the environment, while intelligent and well-guided capitalism is good for all.

Much like simplicity, the notion of sustainability, whose origins have been traced back to the early sixteenth century, has been snatched up by marketers to increase the retail value of some products. It has also been exploited by economists to launch new capitalist ventures.[3] To be sure, sustainability has translated into noticeable changes in purchasing habits and environmentally conscious lifestyles in most Western countries. To take one example, more and more people buy local products to reduce their carbon footprint. As a result of a greater awareness of the environmental risks caused by heedless consumerism, the number of farmers' markets has increased in the United States and the United Kingdom in the last ten years. In addition to assisting with environmental issues, local markets are often presented as a solution to the lack of healthier food and products in underprivileged areas, the so-called 'food deserts'. However, studies have shown that farmers' markets do not begin to address socio-economic disparities in healthy food.[4] They remain a white, middle-class phenomenon with little impact on food justice.

Additionally, locally sourced produce, although generally beneficial for the environment, distracts from a simple reality: it is easy to grow one's own food, even in very small spaces. Thankfully, urban agriculture is on the rise. City planners are opening up to the idea of including urban farms in new planning strategies. If urban agriculture was encouraged and became part of the new city landscape, the effect on healthy food equality would probably be positive.[5] Suburban communities, long seen as the stronghold of environmental ignorance, are being studied as possible locales of ethical farming opportunities, smarter environmental change and planned 'degrowth'.[6] The Transition Town movement, a grass-roots initiative to curtail climate change, to steer public sentiment away from consumerism and to stabilize local economies, is gaining new ground. Much is being done but much more has yet to be accomplished. The 2018 UN International Panel on Climate Change (IPCC) sounded the alarm with its call for urgent change.

While some of the main ideas grouped under the banners of sustainability and frugality manifest themselves in everyday simple living, many staunch simplifiers have criticized the implementation of so-called sustainable economic models that retain growth as their core principle. Degrowth as an economic model offers more viable directions. One of its founding texts, Nicholas Georgescu-Roegen's *The Entropy Law and the Economic Process* (1971) opened the way for a larger diffusion of new growth theories. Serge Latouche has been one of the most vocal promoters of degrowth. Degrowth partisans object to economic growth for its own sake. The projected outcome of degrowth is not infinite economic and consumerist regression but an alternative society that would be ecologically sustainable and socially equitable. According to Latouche, the success of degrowth depends in large part on the decolonization of the imagination from economic imperialism. Freeing minds from the idea of growth as natural and inevitable would allow new societal models and new relationships with the natural world to emerge.[7] Latouche is right to suggest the term 'a-growth' (*a-croissance*), modelled after the term 'atheism', to convey the main ideas behind the movement.[8] Indeed, degrowth asks for the rejection of firmly held beliefs in growth. On the social level, the degrowth programme translates into an increase in modes of exchange which are considered alternative, such as bartering and gifting. Such departures from the current modes of exchange would result in increased social justice, conviviality and happiness. Moreover, degrowth as a global phenomenon proposes to remain mindful of local particulars, whether ecological, social or economic. Decisions on the pace and outcomes of degrowth efforts need to be relevant to the locality. Prosperity for all constitutes the objective of degrowth.

Degrowth as a way of life and as a domestic economic concept has been endorsed by many simplifiers who were already living simple lives. In many respects, the ideas it promotes are in line with Voluntary Simplicity and similar movements. Is 'degrowth' just another word for a millennia-old concept that guided the lives of the Cynics in antiquity, the monks of early Christianity, Quakers and Shakers in early modern Europe and America, philosophers like Rousseau and Thoreau, and the many living in intentional communities governed by frugality, care and simplicity? The idea of degrowth has perhaps remobilized existing forces, and in many ways it has given a new name to an old practice, but probably because it is misunderstood as too radical, it is failing to recruit new people. Degrowth has the merit of capturing the obsession of *homo economicus* with growth, but the term itself may hinder the distribution of the message. By adding a prefix to the obsession that it combats, the word 'degrowth' may expose the movement to the risk of immediate rejection by those addicted to growth. Banners with messages such as 'slow living' are more readily taken up. As an example, the growing success of the Slow Movement promoted in Carl Honoré's *In Praise of Slow* (2004) confirms the hypothesis that pre-packaged ways of life are more willingly accepted today than theories that sound suspiciously academic:

> Fast and Slow do more than just describe a rate of change. They are shorthand for ways of being, or philosophies of life. Fast is busy, controlling, aggressive, hurried, analytical, stressed, superficial, impatient, active, quantity-over-quality. Slow is the opposite: calm, careful, receptive, still, intuitive, unhurried, patient, reflective, quality-over-quantity. It is about making real and meaningful connections – with people, culture, work, food, everything . . . the Slow philosophy can be summed up in a single word: balance.[9]

This passage from *In Praise of Slow* spells out the recipe for the commercial success of an idea: it offers to 'do more' and it whips up a whole philosophy of life complete with binaries – rights and wrongs, good and bad – and quick fixes to big problems. Mostly, it can be reduced to one generally positive word – here, 'balance'. The message: by slowing down, one does more, sees more, feels more, lives more fully. In essence, slow living perpetuates the myth of growth and efficiency, making it more palatable. Degrowth is a simple remedy with a bite; it is not a sugar-coated electuary like the many iterations of the Slow Movement.

As an economic theory and a way of life, degrowth has not yet ousted the idea of growth in dominant political, academic or public discourses, even in those claiming to prioritize the environment and the simple life. In reality, it is proving difficult to combat growth within a culture that has been sustaining it for decades. Looking elsewhere for ideas untainted by our own myths has long interested simplifiers. The syncretic views of Thoreau and Merton, both influenced by Eastern philosophies, are but two examples. New paradigms for degrowth and simple living are also emerging from indigenous Andean cosmologies and their incorporation into the state constitutions of Ecuador and Bolivia. Regional differences notwithstanding, *Sumak Kawsay* in Quechua, *ñandereko* in Guaraní, *Suma Qamaña* in Aymara, *Shiir waras* in Ashuar and *Küme Mongen* in Mapuche all convey the idea of living in harmony with others and with nature. They are translated into Spanish as *Buen Vivir* or *Vivir Bien*, which are rendered into English as 'good way of living' or 'good living'. 'Collective well living' has also been proposed.[10] Like simple living, *Buen Vivir* covers a vast semantic territory that no compound term can capture. It has nevertheless been defined as 'living in plenitude, knowing how to live in harmony with the cycles of Mother Earth, of the cosmos, of life and of history, and in balance with every form of existence in a state of permanent respect'.[11] Advocates of *Buen Vivir* oppose the appropriation of *Pachamama*, Mother Earth, either by anthropomorphic discourses or actual land confiscation orchestrated by insatiable international corporations. *Buen Vivir* acts as a counterforce against forms of economic and cultural colonialism, both established and new. The harmonious mutualism of all living beings, animate or inanimate, at the core of *Buen Vivir* found its way into anticolonial and political discourses first, and later into the constitutions. The impact of economic development on indigenous populations and the environment catalysed a socio-political movement whose voice was increasingly heard in the 2000s. The new Ecuadorian Constitution of 2008, inspired by the principles of *Buen Vivir*, granted rights to nature itself and expanded social justice and equality. Critics point to its co-optation by socialist governments to satisfy their agendas. But the strength of *Buen Vivir* lies in the comprehensiveness of its goals. As a worldview founded on the mutual interconnectedness of all, it defies stable intellectual categories. For Eduardo Gudynas, 'it is not a static concept, but an idea that is continually being created'.[12] A heterogenous set of political and social principles generally antithetical to Western modernity, *Buen Vivir* should not be evaluated on the basis of a few implementations but on the challenges it presents to the imagination, as colonized by Eurocentric politics.

Investigations into the history of simple living reveal that its ideological contours are fluid, its interpretations varied and its manifestations wide-ranging. Much like *Buen Vivir*, simple living federates a range of positions, ideas and ways of living one's life.

As a host concept with far-reaching resonance, simple living cannot be reduced to a set of static principles, lofty ambitions or technological expedients. Simple living can, however, awaken dormant imaginations; it can weaken the force of habit. Simple living offers suggestions for being in the world to those willing to listen to the still small voice of life emitted by all and echoed in all.

REFERENCES

INTRODUCTION

1 Friedrich Nietzsche, 'The Wanderer and His Shadow', in *Human All-Too-Human*, trans. Paul V. Cohn (London, 1934), vol. II, p. 294.

2 Mark C. Taylor, *The Moment of Complexity: Emerging Network Culture* (Chicago, IL, 2003), p. 3.

3 Roland Barthes, *Le Neutre, cours au collège de France (1977–1978)*, ed. Thomas Clerc (Paris, 2002), p. 31.

4 André Comte-Sponville, *A Small Treatise on the Great Virtues*, trans. Catherine Temerson (New York, 2001), pp. 152–3.

5 Jack Cohen and Ian Stewart, *The Collapse of Chaos: Discovering Simplicity in a Complex World* (London, 1995), p. 228.

6 Isaac Newton, *Newton's Principia: The Mathematical Principles of Natural Philosophy*, trans. Andrew Motte (New York, 1846), p. 384.

7 Quoted in John L. Heilbron, 'Wit and Wisdom', *Nature*, CDLXXXIII/3 (2005), p. 29.

8 Gaston Bachelard, *The New Scientific Spirit*, trans. Arthur Goldhammer (Boston, MA, 1984), p. 148.

9 'Simplicity is not a state of things but a state of mind.' Gaston Bachelard, *Essai sur la connaissance rapprochée* (Paris, 1969), p. 98 (translation mine).

10 Lawrence B. Slobodkin, *Simplicity and Complexity in the Games of the Intellect* (Cambridge, MA, 1992), p. 17.

11 See, for instance, Peter A. van der Helm, *Simplicity in Vision: A Multidisciplinary Account of Perceptual Organization* (Cambridge, 2014).

12 Aristotle, *Politics*, in *The Complete Works of Aristotle*, ed. Jonathan Barnes (Oxford, 1995), vol. II, book I, 1252b30.

13 Ibid., 1278b21–30.

14 Giorgio Agamben, *Homo Sacer: Sovereign Power and Bare Life* (Stanford, CA, 1998), p. 9.

15 François Jullien, *The Philosophy of Living*, trans. Michael Richardson and Krzysztof Fijalkowski (London, 2016), p. 161.

16 Ibid., pp. 161–2.

17 See 'sem' and 'plek' in *American Heritage Dictionary of the English Language*, www.thefreedictionary.com, accessed 1 August 2018.

18 One modern example would be the Bach Remedies developed in the early twentieth century and based on the principle of simplicity. See 'On Simplicity' at www.bachcentre.com.

19 *Goethe's Letters to Zelter*, ed. Arthur Duke Coleridge (London, 1892), pp. 282–3.

ONE SIMPLE BEGINNINGS

1 Plato, *Phaedrus*, in *Plato: Complete Works*, ed. John M. Cooper (Indianapolis, IN, and Cambridge, MA, 1997), 274e. All references of works by Plato to this edition.

2 Ibid., 275b.

3 Ibid., 275c.

4 'Dodona', *Oxford Classical Dictionary*, ed. Simon Hornblower, Antony Spawforth and Esther Eidinow (Oxford, 2012).

5 Philostratus, *Images*, trans. Arthur Fairbanks (London, 1931), Book II, 33, p. 267.

6 Plato, *Phaedrus*, 275e.

7 Ibid., 276a.

8 Ibid.

9 Ibid., 276e.

10 Ibid., 277b–c.

11 Jacques Derrida, *Dissemination* (London, 1981), p. 127.

12 Ibid., pp. 125–6.

13 Ibid., p. 126.

14 Ibid., p. 128.

15 Ben Jonson, *Cynthia's Revels* (Dumfries and Galloway, 2017), p. 112.

16 Koen De Temmerman, *Crafting Characters: Heroes and Heroines in the Ancient Greek Novel* (Oxford, 2014), p. 119.

17 Aristotle, *Metaphysics*, in *The Complete Works of Aristotle*, ed. Jonathan Barnes (Oxford, 1995), vol. II, book I, 983b6–27. All references of works by Aristotle to this edition.

18 Ibid., book I, 984a5–6.

19 Ibid., book I, 984a9–11.

20 Parmenides of Elea, *Early Greek Philosophy*, ed. John Burnet (London, 1920), fragment 8, p. 175. A discussion on the nature of Parmenides' monism is beyond the scope of this chapter.

21 Plato, *Theaetetus*, 180e.

22 Ibid., 184a.

23 Plato, *Phaedo*, 100d–e.

24 See Plato, *Timaeus*, 27d–28a and 37e–38a, *Phaedrus*, 247c.

25 See *Phaedo*, 80b, on the immortality of the soul vs the mortality of the body. 'Consider then, Cebes, whether it follows from all that has been said that the soul is most like the divine, deathless, intelligible, uniform, indissoluble, always the same as itself, whereas the body is most like that which is human, mortal, multiform, unintelligible, soluble, and never consistently the same.'

26 Plotinus, *The Enneads*, trans. Stephen MacKenna (London, 1956), V, 2, 1.

27 Ibid., II, 9, 1.

28 Ibid.

29 Ibid., VI, 9, 4.

30 Ibid., VI, 9, 7.

31 Ibid., VI, 9, 11.

32 Ibid.

33 Ibid.

34 Ibid., II, 9, 14.

35 Ibid.

36 Blaise Pascal, *Pensées*, trans. Roger Ariew (Indianapolis, IN, and Cambridge, 2004), p. 144. (Sellier 457 and Lafuma 533).

37 See for instance Pierre Hadot, *Philosophy as a Way of Life: Spiritual Exercises from Socrates to Foucault* (Oxford, 1995).

38 Friedrich Nietzsche, 'The Wanderer and His Shadow', in *Human All-Too-Human*, trans. Paul V. Cohn (London, 1911), vol. II, ch. 196, p. 294.

39 Ibid., vol. II, ch. 86, p. 245.

40 Xenophon, *Memorabilia*, trans. E. C. Marchand (London, 1923), book I, 6, 2–3.

41 Ibid., book I, 6 ,10.

42 Ibid., 6, 14.

43 Ibid.

44 Plato, *Republic*, VI, 485e.

45 Ibid., III, 416e.

46 Ibid., II, 372b–d.

47 Ibid., 361b.

48 Ibid., IV, 427e.

49 Ibid., 431c.

50 Aristotle, *Nicomachean Ethics*, book I, 10, 1101a15–16.

51 Ibid., 1100b25–26.

52 Aristotle, *Politics*, book I, 10, 1258b2–3.

53 Ibid., book II, 3, 1261b33–34.

54 Karen Margrethe Nielsen, 'Economy and Private Property', in *The Cambridge Companion to Aristotle's Politics*, ed. M. Deslauriers and P. Destrée (Cambridge, 2013), p. 84.

55 Marcus Aurelius, *Meditations*, trans. Gregory Hays (New York, 2003), book I, 3.

56 Ibid., book XI, 15.

57 Ibid., book VI, 13.

58 Dio Chrysostom, *Discourses*, trans. J. W. Cohoon (Cambridge, MA, 1932), vol. I, discourse 6, 28.

59 Diogenes Laërtius, *Lives of Eminent Philosophers*, trans R. D. Hicks (Cambridge, MA, 1931), vol. II, book 6, p. 39.

60 William Desmond, *Cynics* (Stocksfield, 2008), pp. 156–7.

61 Julian, *Oration* 6.187c–d. Quoted in Desmond, *Cynics*, p. 15.

62 Saint Jerome, 'Against Jovinianus', in *The Principal Works of St Jerome*, trans. W. H. Fremantle (Oxford, 1893), vol. VI, book II, 14, p. 846.

63 Ibid., p. 847.

64 André-François Boureau-Deslandes, *Histoire critique de la philosophie* (Amsterdam, 1737), vol. II, p. 188.

65 Ibid.

66 Ibid., pp. 192–3.

TWO WALKING IN SIMPLICITY

1 King James Version (KJV). This is the translation of the Vulgate, which reads, 'Job . . . erat vir ille simplex et rectus.'

2 Ceslas Spicq, 'La Vertu de simplicité dans l'Ancien et le Nouveau Testament', *Revue des sciences philosophiques et théologiques*, XXII/1 (1933), p. 7.

3 'Moriamur omnes in simplicitate nostra' (1 Macc 2:37). Translation mine.

4 'Scio, Deus meus, quod probes corda, et simplicitatem diligas, unde et

ego in simplicitate cordis mei laetus obtuli universa haec: et populum tuum qui hic repertus est, vidi cum ingenti gaudio tibi offere donaria.' 1 Chronicles 29:17.

5 Romans 12:6–8, Authorized King James Version (AKJV).

6 Wisdom of Solomon 1:1–2. King James Version with Apocrypha (KJVA).

7 Testament of Issachar, in *Ante-Nicene Fathers: The Writings of the Fathers down to AD 325* (New York, 1903), vol. VIII, p. 22.

8 Issacher 3:8, ibid.

9 Issacher 4:1–6, ibid.

10 Issacher 5:1–4, ibid.

11 Issacher 6:1, ibid.

12 Ibid., p. 23.

13 Issacher 7:7, ibid.

14 'The Shepherd of Hermas', in *The Apostolic Fathers*, trans. Joseph Barber Lightfoot (New York, 1891), p. 409.

15 Ibid., p. 458.

16 Ibid., p. 475.

17 Oscar J. F. Seitz, 'Afterthoughts on the Term "Dipsychos"', *New Testament Studies*, IV/4 (1958), pp. 327–34.

18 David A. Michelson, *The Practical Christology of Philoxenos of Mabbug* (Oxford, 2014), pp. 2–3.

19 *The Discourses of Philoxenos of Mabbug*, trans. Robert A. Kitchen (Collegeville, MN, 2013), p. 64.

20 Ibid., p. 56.

21 David A. Michelson, 'Philoxenos of Mabbug and the Simplicity of Evagrian Gnosis: Competing Uses of Evagrius in the Early Sixth Century', in *Evagrius and His Legacy*, ed. Joel Kalvesmaki and Robin Darling Young (South Bend, IN, 2016), pp. 175–205.

22 Michelson, *Practical Christology*, p. 196.

23 Philoxenos, *Discourses*, pp. 96–7.

24 Ibid., p. 99.

25 Ibid., p. 103.

26 Ibid., p. 104.

27 Ibid., p. 106.

28 Ibid., pp. 107–8.

29 Ibid., pp. 110–11. Emphasis mine.

30 Ibid., p. 111.

31 Ibid., p. 112.

32 Ibid., p. 116.

33 Ibid., p. 117.
34 Ibid., p. 116.
35 Ibid., p. 119.
36 Ibid.
37 Michelson, *Practical Christology*, p. 21.
38 Philoxenos, *Discourses*, p. 180.
39 Ibid., pp. 205–6.
40 Ibid., p. 344.
41 Ibid., p. 359.
42 Ibid., p. 360.
43 Ibid., pp. 366–7.
44 Giorgio Agamben, *The Highest Poverty: Monastic Rules and Form-of-life* (Stanford, CA, 2013), p. xi.
45 Thomas Merton, *Zen and the Birds of Appetite* (New York, 1968), pp. 61–2.
46 Ibid., p. 62.
47 Thomas Keating, 'The Seven Stages of Centering Prayer', *Contemplative Outreach News*, XXVIII/2 (2012), p. 2.
48 Thomas Keating, 'Simplicity', *Contemplative Outreach News*, XXVIII/1 (2011), p. 1.
49 Ibid.
50 Ibid.
51 Ibid.
52 Jean-Baptiste Chautard, *The Spirit of Simplicity*, trans. Thomas Merton (Notre Dame, IN, 2017), pp. 79–80.
53 Ibid., pp. 93–4.
54 Ibid., p. 94.
55 Ibid., p. 98.
56 Ibid.
57 Ibid., p. 109.
58 Ibid., pp. 109–10.
59 Ibid., p. 110.
60 Ibid., p. 105.
61 Gordon Oyer, 'Thomas Merton and the "Pessimism" of Jacques Ellul', *Merton Annual*, XXX (2017), pp. 131–44.
62 Ibid., pp. 140–41.
63 Thomas Merton, *Turning toward the World: The Pivotal Years, Journals, vol. IV: 1960–1963*, ed. Victor A. Kramer (San Francisco, CA, 1996), p. 11.
64 Ibid., p. 10.

65 Jacques Ellul, *The Technological Society* (New York, 1964), p. xxv.

66 Ibid., p. 325.

67 Jacques Ellul, 'Technique and the Opening Chapter of Genesis', in *Theology and Technology: Essays in Christian Analysis and Exegesis*, ed. and trans. Carl Mitcham and Jim Grote (Lanham, MD, 1984), pp. 126–7.

68 Ibid., p. 135.

69 Ibid., p. 128.

70 Ibid., p. 129.

71 Ibid.

THREE THE 'GIFT TO BE SIMPLE'

1 Quoted in Edward Deming Andrews, *The Gift to Be Simple: Songs, Dances and Rituals of the American Shakers* (New York, 1962), p. 136.

2 Ibid., p. 67. The song was composed by 'Henry B.' and is dated 10 October 1843.

3 Ibid., p. 113.

4 Stephen J. Stein, *The Shaker Experience in America: A History of the United Society of Believers* (New Haven, CT, and London, 1992), p. 173.

5 Ibid., p. 185.

6 *Summary View of the Millennial Church* (Albany, NY, 1823), pp. 248–9. Emphases mine.

7 Ibid., p. 253.

8 Ibid., p. 268.

9 Ibid., p. 266.

10 Laura Paine, 'Hands to Work, Hearts to God: The Story of the Shaker Seed Industry', *HortTechnology*, III/4 (1993), pp. 375–82.

11 Quoted in Flo Morse, *The Shakers and the World's People* (New York, 1980), p. 184.

12 Quoted ibid., p. 266.

13 Quoted in Christian Becksvoort, *The Shaker Legacy: Perspectives on an Enduring Furniture Style* (Newtown, CT, 2000), p. 2.

14 Ibid., pp. 18–19.

15 'Simple Gifts: Shaker at The Met', www.metmuseum.org, accessed 1 November 2017.

16 See www.shakerdesignproject.com, accessed 1 November 2017.

17 Quoted in Becksvoort, *The Shaker Legacy*, p. 16.

18 Morse, *The Shakers*, p. 115.

19 Quoted ibid., p. 349.

20 See Morse, *The Shakers*, p. 182.

21 Anne Midgette, 'Music Review: John Williams's "Air and Simple Gifts" at the Obama Inauguration', www.washingtonpost.com, 21 January 2009.

22 Frederick William Evans, *Shakers Compendium*, 4th edn (New Lebanon, NY, 1867), pp. 18–20.

23 Marie Huber, *The World Unmask'd; or, The Philosopher the Greatest Cheat* (London, 1736), p. 95.

24 James Nayler, *A Collection of Sundry Books, Epistles and Papers* (London, 1716), p. iv, p. xxi and p. xxvi.

25 Ibid., pp. 258–9.

26 Ibid., p. 259.

27 Ibid., p. xxvi.

28 Ibid., p. 261.

29 Ibid., p. 385.

30 Ibid., p. 271.

31 Ibid., p. 397.

32 William Penn, *No Cross, No Crown* (Leeds, 1743), p. 94.

33 Ibid., p. 208.

34 Ibid.

35 Ibid., pp. 208–9.

36 Ibid., p. 209.

37 Robert Barclay, *An Apology for the True Christian Divinity* (London, 1780), p. 538.

38 Ibid., p. 540.

39 John Woolman, *The Journal of John Woolman* (Gloucester, MA, 1971), p. vii.

40 Ibid., pp. 8–9.

41 Ibid., p. 205.

42 Ibid., p. 163.

43 Anthony Benezet, *Observations on Plainness and Simplicity* (n.p., n.d.), p. 6.

44 Ibid., p. 7.

45 Ibid., p. 8.

46 Elias Hicks, *Journal of the Life and Religious Labours of Elias Hicks* (New York, 1832), p. 62 and p. 91.

47 Ibid., p. 353.

48 Ibid., p. 162.

49 Ibid., p. 449.

50 Quoted in Kenneth L. Carroll, 'Early Quakers and "Going Naked as a Sign"', *Quaker History*, LXVII/2 (1978), p. 76.

51 William Craig Brownlee, *A Careful and Free Inquiry into the True Nature and Tendency of the Religious Principles of the Society of Friends* (Philadelphia, PA, 1824), p. 96.

52 Marcus Rediker, *The Fearless Benjamin Lay* (Boston, MA, 2017), p. 2.

53 Ibid., p. 149.

54 Ibid., p. 101.

55 Ibid.

FOUR A SIMPLE REFORM

1 Jean-Jacques Rousseau, 'The Reveries of the Solitary Walker', in *The Collected Writings of Rousseau*, ed. Christopher Kelly (Hanover, NH, and London, 2000), vol. VIII, pp. 19–20.

2 Jean-Jacques Rousseau, 'Rousseau Judge of Jean-Jacques: Dialogues', in *The Collected Writings of Rousseau*, ed. Roger D. Masters and Christopher Kelly (Hanover, NH, and London, 1990), vol. I, pp. 132–3.

3 Jean-Jacques Rousseau, 'Discourse on the Origins of Inequality', in *The Collected Writings of Rousseau*, ed. Roger D. Masters and Christopher Kelly (Hanover, NH, and London, 1992), vol. III, p. 13.

4 Jean-Jacques Rousseau, 'Emile, or on Education', in *The Collected Writings of Rousseau*, ed. Christopher Kelly and Allan Bloom (Hanover, NH, and London, 2010), vol. XIII, p. 591.

5 Ibid., p. 592.

6 *Jean-Jacques Rousseau et Henriette*, ed. Hippolyte Buffenoir (Paris, 1902), p. 17. Translation mine.

7 Ibid., p. 38. Translation mine.

8 Ibid., p. 40. Translation mine.

9 Rousseau, 'Discourse on Inequality', p. 26.

10 Taken from Pierre Burgelin, *La Philosophie de l'existence de Jean-Jacques Rousseau* (Paris, 1973), p. 272.

11 Rousseau, 'Discourse on Inequality', pp. 20–21.

12 Ibid., pp. 70–71.

13 Ibid., p. 21.

14 Ibid., p. 12.

15 Ibid.

16 Ibid., p. 43.

17 Jean-Jacques Rousseau, 'Political Fragments', in *The Collected Writings*

of Rousseau, ed. Roger D. Masters and Christopher Kelly (Hanover, NH, and London, 1994), vol. IV, p. 18. In fragment 1, Rousseau wrote: 'Anyone who, renouncing in good faith all the prejudices of human vanity, will reflect seriously on all these things will find in the end that all the noble words of society, justice, laws, mutual defense, assistance to the weak, philosophy, and progress of reason, are only lures invented by clever political thinkers or cowardly flatterers in order to deceive the simple-minded.' Ibid., p. 17. Rousseau used the noun *'les simples'*, which is not as pejorative as the English, 'the simple-minded'.

18 Rousseau, 'Discourse on Inequality', p. 79.

19 Ibid., p. 80.

20 Jean-Jacques Rousseau, 'Social Contract', in *The Collected Writings of Rousseau*, vol. IV, p. 198.

21 Ibid., p. 190. In this translation, the French *simple* is rendered as 'single' in English.

22 Ibid., p. 180.

23 Ibid.

24 Jean-Jacques Rousseau, 'Julie or the New Heloise', in *The Collected Writings of Rousseau*, trans. Philip Stewart and Jean Vaché (Hanover, NH, and London, 1997), vol. VI, p. 153. 'I was trying in this way to turn aside his grim thoughts with that of a familiar correspondence maintained between us, and that simple soul who seeks only, so to speak, to latch onto what surrounds you, easily took the bait.'

25 Rousseau, 'Discourse on Inequality', p. 23.

26 Ibid., p. 23.

27 Rousseau, 'Social Contract', p. 77.

28 Louis Althusser, *Cours sur Rousseau* (Paris, 2012).

29 Rousseau, 'Emile', p. 343.

30 Ibid., p. 342.

31 Rousseau, 'Julie', p. 32.

32 Rousseau, 'Emile', p. 474.

33 Ibid., p. 474.

34 Rousseau, 'Discourse on Inequality', p. 42.

35 Rousseau, 'Emile', p. 475.

36 Ibid.

37 Henry David Thoreau, 'Walden', in *Henry David Thoreau*, ed. Robert F. Sayre (New York, 1985), p. 325.

38 Ibid., p. 327.

39 Ibid., p. 334.

40 Ibid.
41 Ibid.
42 Ibid., p. 394.
43 Ibid., p. 395.
44 Ibid.
45 Ibid., p. 373.
46 Ibid.
47 Giorgio Agamben, *Profanations* (New York, 2015), p. 82.
48 Thoreau, 'Walden', p. 373.
49 Charles Frederick Briggs, 'A Yankee Diogenes', *Putnam's Monthly*, IV (1854), p. 443.
50 Ibid.
51 Henry David Thoreau, 'Life without Principle', *Atlantic Monthly*, XII (1863), p. 487.
52 Ibid.
53 Ibid.
54 Ibid.
55 Ibid., p. 488.
56 Ibid.
57 Ralph Waldo Emerson, 'Spiritual Laws', in *The Complete Works of Ralph Waldo Emerson*, ed. Edward Waldo Emerson (Boston, MA, and New York, 1903–4), vol. II, p. 137.
58 Ralph Waldo Emerson, 'Literary Ethics', ibid., vol. I, p. 165.
59 Ibid., pp. 165–6.
60 Ralph Waldo Emerson, 'Natural History of the Intellect', ibid., vol. XII, p. 63.
61 Ralph Waldo Emerson, 'Self-reliance', ibid., vol. II, p. 66.
62 Ibid., pp. 66–7.
63 Ibid., p. 69.
64 Ibid.
65 Ibid., p. 70.
66 Ralph Waldo Emerson, 'The Transcendentalist', ibid., vol. I, p. 334.
67 See Richard Francis, *Fruitlands: The Alcott Family and Their Search for Utopia* (New Haven, CT, 2010).
68 Quoted in Matthew Jefferies, '*Lebensreform*: A Middle-class Antidote to Wilhelminism?', in *Wilhelminism and Its Legacies: German Modernities, Imperialism, and the Meanings of Reform, 1890–1930*, ed. Geoff Eley and James Retallack (Oxford and New York, 2003), p. 91.
69 Ibid., p. 98.

70 Ibid., p. 97.
71 Susan Okie, 'Getting a Profile of Health Store Customers',
    Washington Post, 5 August 1997, p. 5.

FIVE SIMPLICITY MADE SIMPLE

1 Walter Benjamin, 'Experience and Poverty', in *Selected Writings*, vol. II:
   1927–1934, trans. Rodney Livingstone and others, ed. Michael W.
   Jennings, Howard Eiland and Gary Smith (Cambridge, MA, 1999),
   p. 732.
2 Ibid., p. 733.
3 Ibid., p. 734.
4 Ibid.
5 Ibid., p. 733.
6 Ibid., p. 734.
7 Alexander Pope, 'Ode on Solitude', in *Complete Poetical Works of
   Alexander Pope*, ed. W. C. Armstrong (New York, 1877), vol. I, p. 329.
8 Henri Bergson, *Les Deux Sources de la morale et de la religion*
   (Paris, 1932), p. 343. Translation mine.
9 Ibid., p. 330.
10 Ibid., p. 332.
11 Ibid., p. 335.
12 See Jean-Christophe Goddard, *Mysticisme et folie: Essai sur la simplicité*
    (Paris, 2002), p. 16.
13 Vladimir Jankélévitch, *L'Innocence et la méchanceté, Traité des vertus*,
    vol. III (Paris, 1986), p. 411.
14 Ibid., p. 420.
15 Ibid., p. 421.
16 Jamie Bartlett, 'Will 2018 Be the Year of the Neo-Luddite?',
    www.guardian.co.uk, 4 March 2018.
17 Jamie Bartlett, *The People vs Tech* (London, 2018), p. 1.
18 Theodore Kaczynski, *Technological Slavery* (Port Townsend, WA, 2008),
    pp. 13–15.
19 Ibid., p. 32.
20 Ibid., pp. 170–71.
21 Samuel Alexander, 'Wild Democracy: A Biodiversity of Resistance
    and Renewal', Simplicity Institute Report 16a (2016),
    www.simplicityinstitute.org, p. 16.
22 Ibid.

23 Ibid., p. 15.

24 Ibid., p. 18.

25 Henry David Thoreau, 'A Week on the Concord and Merrimack Rivers', in *Henry David Thoreau*, ed. Robert F. Sayre (New York, 1985), p. 238.

26 Martin Heidegger, 'The Question Concerning Technology', in *The Question Concerning Technology and Other Essays*, ed. William Lovitt (New York, 1977), p. 13.

27 Ibid., p. 14.

28 Ibid., p. 17.

29 Ibid., p. 18.

30 Ibid.

31 Ibid., p. 27.

32 Ibid., p. 28.

33 Ibid., p. 34.

34 Martin Heidegger, *What Is Called Thinking?*, trans. J. Glenn Gray (New York, 1968), pp. 14–15.

35 Clément Rosset, *The Real and Its Double*, trans. Chris Turner (Calcutta, 2012), p. 3.

36 Ibid., p. 24.

37 Ibid., p. vii.

38 Ibid., pp. 43–4.

39 Ibid., pp. ix–x.

40 Ibid., p. xvi.

41 Ibid., p. 19.

42 Clément Rosset, *Le Réel: Traité de l'idiotie* (Paris, 1997), p. 21.

43 Ibid., p. 29.

44 Rosset, *The Real*, p. 45. Rosset uses the term 'humiliation'. Humiliation is a debasement of the social self, which is explained later.

45 Clément Rosset, *Loin de moi* (Paris, 1999), pp. 35–7.

46 Ibid., p. 39.

47 Ibid., pp. 43–4.

48 Ibid., pp. 50–51.

49 Ibid., p. 89.

50 Richard B. Gregg, *The Value of Voluntary Simplicity* (Wallingford, PA, 1936), p. 4.

51 Samuel Alexander and Simon Ussher, 'The Voluntary Simplicity Movement: A Multi-national Survey Analysis in Theoretical Context', *Journal of Consumer Culture*, XII/1 (2012), pp. 66–86.

52 Ibid., p. 73.

53 Ibid.
54 Ibid., p. 74.
55 Ibid.
56 Ibid., p. 78.
57 Ibid., p. 76.
58 Ibid., p. 77.
59 Ibid., p. 79.
60 Ibid.
61 Patrick Spenner and Karen Freeman, 'To Keep Your Customers, Keep It Simple', *Harvard Business Review* (May 2012), pp. 109–14.
62 Ibid., p. 110.
63 Ibid.
64 Ibid.
65 Ken Segall, *Insanely Simple: The Obsession That Drives Apple's Success* (New York, 2012), p. 3.
66 Ibid.
67 Ibid., p. 4.
68 Ibid., p. 5.
69 Ibid.
70 Ibid., p. 4.
71 Ibid., p. 5.
72 Ibid.
73 Ibid., p. 7.
74 Donald Trump, *The Art of the Deal* (New York, 1987), pp. 45–8.
75 Daniel Kahneman, *Thinking, Fast and Slow* (London, 2012), p. 12.
76 Ibid., p. 45.
77 Ibid., p. 85.
78 Jacob Feldman, 'How Surprising Is a Simple Pattern? Quantifying "Eureka"', *Cognition*, XCIII (2004), p. 218.
79 Adrian Dimulescu and Jean-Louis Dessalles, 'Understanding Narrative Interest: Some Evidence on the Role of Unexpectedness', *Proceedings of the 31st Annual Conference of the Cognitive Science Society* (Amsterdam, 2009), pp. 1737–8. Available online at www.csjarchive.cogsci.rpi.edu.
80 Giovanni Sileno, Antoine Saillenfest and Jean-Louis Dessalles, 'A Computational Model of Moral and Legal Responsibility via Simplicity Theory', *Jurix 2017*, ed. A. Wyner and G. Casini, p. 173. Available online at https://jurix2017.gforge.uni.lu.
81 Antoine Saillenfest, Jean-Louis Dessalles and Olivier Auber, 'Role of

Simplicity in Creative Behaviour: The Case of the Poietic Generator',
*Proceedings of the Seventh International Conference on Computational
Creativity*, ed. F. Pachet, A. Cardoso, V. Corruble and F. Ghedini (2016),
p. 34. Available online at www.computationalcreativity.net.

82 Alexander and Ussher, 'The Voluntary Simplicity Movement', p. 82.

83 Amitai Etzioni, 'Voluntary Simplicity: Characterization, Select
Psychological Implications, and Societal Consequences', *Journal of
Economic Psychology*, XIX (1998), pp. 619–43. In Etzioni's typology,
simplifiers are ranked according to their degree of commitment, starting
with the downshifters, then the strong simplifiers and finally those who
have joined the simple living movements.

84 Alexandra Hüttel et al., 'To Purchase or Not? Why Consumers Make
Economically (Non-) Sustainable Consumption Choices', *Journal of
Cleaner Production*, CLXXIV (2018), p. 833.

85 Mathias Peyer, Ingo Balderjahn, Barbara Seegebarth and Alexandra
Klemm, 'The Role of Sustainability in Profiling Voluntary Simplifiers',
Journal of Business Research, LXX (2017), pp. 41–2.

CONCLUSION

1 Quoted in 'Prince Charles at 70: Is This Multimillionaire Really a Role
Model for Frugality?', www.guardian.co.uk, accessed 14 November 2018.

2 See www.princeofwales.gov.uk/sustainability, accessed 19 November
2018.

3 See Paul Warde, *The Invention of Sustainability: Nature and Destiny,
c. 1500–1870* (Cambridge, 2018); Jeremy Caradonna, *Sustainability:
A History* (Oxford, 2014) and Ulrich Grober, *Sustainability: A Cultural
History* (Totnes, 2012).

4 See for instance the following study of farmers' markets in Los Angeles:
Bryce Lowery et al., 'Do Farmers' Markets Increase Access to Healthy
Foods for All Communities? Comparing Markets in 24 Neighborhoods
in Los Angeles', *Journal of the American Planning Association*, LXXXII/3
(2016), pp. 252–66.

5 See for instance, Megan Horst, Nathan McClintock and Lesli Hoey,
'The Intersection of Planning, Urban Agriculture, and Food Justice:
A Review of the Literature', *Journal of the American Planning Association*,
LXXXIII/3 (2017), pp. 277–95.

6 Samuel Alexander and Brendan Gleeson, *Degrowth in the Suburbs:
A Radical Urban Imaginary* (London, 2018).

7 Serge Latouche, *Les Précurseurs de la décroissance: Une anthologie* (Neuvy-en-Champagne, 2016), p. 19.

8 Ibid., p. 10.

9 Carl Honoré, *In Praise of Slow: How a Worldwide Movement Is Challenging the Cult of Speed* (London, 2004), p. 13.

10 Daniela Bressa Florentin, 'Between Policies and Life: The Political Process of Buen Vivir in Ecuador', in *The Politics of Wellbeing: Theory, Policy and Practice*, ed. Ian Bache and Karen Scott (London, 2018), pp. 121–42.

11 Quoted in Julien Vanhulst and Adrian E. Beling, '*Buen vivir*: Emergent Discourse within or beyond Sustainable Development?', *Ecological Economics*, CI (May 2014), p. 56.

12 Eduardo Gudynas, 'Buen Vivir: Today's Tomorrow', *Development*, LIV/4 (2011), p. 443.

BIBLIOGRAPHY

Agamben, Giorgio, *The Highest Poverty: Monastic Rules and Form-of-life*
(Stanford, CA, 2013)
——, *Homo Sacer, Sovereign Power and Bare Life* (Stanford, CA, 1998)
——, *Profanations* (New York, 2015)
Alexander, Samuel, and Brendan Gleeson, *Degrowth in the Suburbs:
A Radical Urban Imaginary* (London, 2018)
Alexander, Samuel, and Amanda McLeod, *Simple Living in History: Pioneers
of the Deep Future* (Melbourne, 2014)
Alexander, Samuel, and Simon Ussher, 'The Voluntary Simplicity
Movement: A Multi-national Survey Analysis in Theoretical Context',
Journal of Consumer Culture, XII/1 (2012), pp. 66–86
Althusser, Louis, *Cours sur Rousseau* (Paris, 2012)
Andrews, Edward Deming, *The Gift to Be Simple: Songs, Dances and Rituals
of the American Shakers* (New York, 1962)
Aristotle, *Metaphysics*, in *The Complete Works of Aristotle*, ed. Jonathan
Barnes (Oxford, 1995), vol. II, pp. 1552–728
——, *Nicomachean Ethics*, ibid., pp. 1729–867
——, *Politics*, ibid., pp. 1986–2129
Bachelard, Gaston, *The New Scientific Spirit*, trans. Arthur Goldhammer
(Boston, MA, 1984)
Barclay, Robert, *An Apology for the True Christian Divinity* (London, 1780)
Barthes, Roland, *Le Neutre: cours au collège de France (1977–1978)*,
ed. Thomas Clerc (Paris, 2002)
Bartlett, Jamie, *The People vs Tech* (London, 2018)
Becksvoort, Christian, *The Shaker Legacy: Perspectives on an Enduring
Furniture Style* (Newtown, CT, 2000)

Benezet, Anthony, *Observations on Plainness and Simplicity* (n.p., n.d.)

Benjamin, Walter, 'Experience and Poverty', in *Selected Writings*, vol. II: *1927–1934*, trans. Rodney Livingstone et al., ed. Michael W. Jennings, Howard Eiland and Gary Smith (Cambridge, MA, 1999), pp. 731–6

Bergson, Henri, *Les Deux Sources de la morale et de la religion* (Paris, 1932)

Brownlee, William Craig, *A Careful and Free Inquiry into the True Nature and Tendency of the Religious Principles of the Society of Friends* (Philadelphia, PA, 1824)

Buffenoir, Hippolyte, ed., *Jean-Jacques Rousseau et Henriette* (Paris, 1902)

Caradonna, Jeremy L., *Sustainability: A History* (Oxford, 2014)

Chautard, Jean-Baptiste, *The Spirit of Simplicity*, trans. Thomas Merton (Notre Dame, IN, 2017)

Cohen, Jack, and Ian Stewart, *The Collapse of Chaos: Discovering Simplicity in a Complex World* (London, 1995)

Comte-Sponville, André, *A Small Treatise on the Great Virtues* (New York, 2001)

de Halleux, André, *Philoxène de Mabbog: sa vie, ses ecrits, sa theologie* (Leuven, 1963)

De Temmerman, Koen, *Crafting Characters: Heroes and Heroines in the Ancient Greek Novel* (Oxford, 2014)

Derrida, Jacques, *Dissemination* (London, 1981)

Desmond, William, *Cynics* (Stocksfield, 2008)

Dio Chrysostom, *Discourses*, trans. J. W. Cohoon (Cambridge, MA, 1932)

Diogenes Laërtius, *Lives of Eminent Philosophers*, trans. Robert Drew Hicks (Cambridge, MA, 1931)

Elgin, Duane, *Voluntary Simplicity: Toward a Way of Life That is Outwardly Simple, Inwardly Rich* (New York, 1993)

Ellul, Jacques, 'Technique and the Opening Chapter of Genesis', in *Theology and Technology: Essays in Christian Analysis and Exegesis*, ed. and trans. Carl Mitcham and Jim Grote (Lanham, MD, 1984)

——, *The Technological Society* (New York, 1964)

Emerson, Ralph Waldo, 'Literary Ethics', in *The Complete Works of Ralph Waldo Emerson*, ed. Edward Waldo Emerson (Boston, MA, and New York, 1903–4), vol. I, pp. 153–87

——, 'Natural History of the Intellect', ibid., vol. XII, pp. 1–110

——, 'Self-reliance', ibid., vol. II, pp. 43–90

——, 'Spiritual Laws', ibid., pp. 129–66

——, 'The Transcendentalist', ibid., vol. I, pp. 327–59

Etzioni, Amitai, 'Voluntary Simplicity: Characterization, Select
    Psychological Implications, and Societal Consequences', *Journal
    of Economic Psychology*, XIX (1998), pp. 619–43
Evans, Frederick William, *Shakers Compendium* (New Lebanon, NY, 1867)
Feldman, Jacob, 'How Surprising Is a Simple Pattern? Quantifying "Eureka"',
    Cognition, XCIII (2004), pp. 199–224
Francis, Richard, *Fruitlands: The Alcott Family and Their Search for Utopia*
    (New Haven, CT, 2010)
Goddard, Jean-Christophe, *Mysticisme et folie: Essai sur la simplicité*
    (Paris, 2002)
Gregg, Richard B., *The Value of Voluntary Simplicity* (Wallingford, PA, 1936)
Grober, Ulrich, *Sustainability: A Cultural History* (Totnes, 2012)
Gudynas, Eduardo, 'Buen Vivir: Today's Tomorrow', *Development*, LIV/4
    (2011), pp. 441–7
Hadot, Pierre, *Philosophy as a Way of Life: Spiritual Exercises from Socrates
    to Foucault* (Oxford, 1995)
Heidegger, Martin, 'The Question Concerning Technology', in *The Question
    Concerning Technology and Other Essays*, ed. William Lovitt
    (New York, 1977), pp. 3–35
—, *What Is Called Thinking?*, trans. J. Glenn Gray (New York, 1968)
Hicks, Elias, *Journal of the Life and Religious Labours of Elias Hicks*
    (New York, 1832)
Honoré, Carl, *In Praise of Slow: How a Worldwide Movement Is Challenging
    the Cult of Speed* (London, 2004)
Huber, Marie, *The World Unmask'd; or, The Philosopher the Greatest Cheat*
    (London, 1736)
Jankélévitch, Vladimir, *Henri Bergson* (Durham, NC, 2015)
—, *L'Innocence et la méchanceté, Traité des vertus*, vol. III (Paris, 1986)
Jonson, Ben, *Cynthia's Revels* (Dumfries and Galloway, 2017)
Jullien, François, *The Philosophy of Living*, trans. Michael Richardson
    and Krzysztof Fijalkowski (London, 2016)
Kaczynski, Theodore, *Technological Slavery* (Port Townsend, WA, 2008)
Kahneman, Daniel, *Thinking, Fast and Slow* (London, 2012)
Keating, Thomas, 'The Seven Stages of Centering Prayer', *Contemplative
    Outreach News*, XXVIII/2 (2012), pp. 1–2
—, 'Simplicity', *Contemplative Outreach News*, XXVIII/1 (2011), p. 1
King James Bible
Latouche, Serge, *Les Précurseurs de la décroissance: Une anthologie*
    (Neuvy-en-Champagne, 2016)

Marcus Aurelius, *Meditations*, trans. Gregory Hays (New York, 2003)

Merton, Thomas, *Turning toward the World: The Pivotal Years. Journals*, vol. IV, *1960–1963*, ed. Victor A. Kramer (San Francisco, CA, 1996)

—, *Zen and the Birds of Appetite* (New York, 1968)

Michelson, David A., *The Practical Christology of Philoxenos of Mabbug* (Oxford, 2014)

Morse, Flo, *The Shakers and the World's People* (New York, 1980)

Nayler, James, *A Collection of Sundry Books, Epistles and Papers* (London, 1716)

Newton, Isaac, *Newton's Principia: The Mathematical Principles of Natural Philosophy*, trans. Andrew Motte (New York, 1846)

Nietzsche, Friedrich, 'The Wanderer and His Shadow', in *Human, All-Too-Human*, trans. Paul V. Cohn (London, 1911)

Pascal, Blaise, *Pensées*, trans. Roger Ariew (Indianapolis, IN, and Cambridge, 2004)

Penn, William, *No Cross, No Crown* (Leeds, 1743)

Philostratus, *Images*, trans. Arthur Fairbanks (London, 1931)

Philoxenos of Mabbug, *The Discourses of Philoxenos of Mabbug*, trans. Robert A. Kitchen (Collegeville, MN, 2013)

Plato, *Phaedo*, in *Plato: Complete Works*, ed. John M. Cooper (Indianapolis, IN, and Cambridge, MA, 1997), pp. 49–100

—, *Phaedrus*, ibid., pp. 506–56

—, *Republic*, ibid., pp. 971–1223

—, *Theaetetus*, ibid., pp. 157–234

Plotinus, *The Enneads*, trans. Stephen MacKenna (London, 1956)

Pope, Alexander, 'Ode on Solitude', in *Complete Poetical Works of Alexander Pope*, ed. W. C. Armstrong (New York, 1877), vol. I

Rediker, Marcus, *The Fearless Benjamin Lay* (Boston, MA, 2017)

Rosset, Clément, *Loin de moi* (Paris, 1999)

—, *The Real and Its Double*, trans. Chris Turner (Calcutta, 2012)

—, *Le Réel: Traité de l'idiotie* (Paris, 1997)

Rousseau, Jean-Jacques, 'Discourse on the Origins of Inequality', in *The Collected Writings of Rousseau*, ed. Roger D. Masters and Christopher Kelly (Hanover, NH, and London, 1992), vol. III

—, 'Emile, or on Education', in *The Collected Writings of Rousseau*, ed. Christopher Kelly and Allan Bloom (Hanover, NH, and London, 2010), vol. XIII

—, 'Julie or the New Heloise', in *The Collected Writings of Rousseau*, trans. Philip Stewart and Jean Vaché (Hanover, NH, and London, 1997), vol. VI

——, 'Political Fragments', in *The Collected Writings of Rousseau*, ed. Roger D. Masters and Christopher Kelly (Hanover, NH, and London, 1994), vol. IV

——, 'The Reveries of the Solitary Walker', in *The Collected Writings of Rousseau*, ed. Christopher Kelly (Hanover, NH, and London, 2000), vol. VIII

——, 'Rousseau Judge of Jean-Jacques: Dialogues', in *The Collected Writings of Rousseau*, ed. Roger D. Masters and Christopher Kelly (Hanover, NH, and London, 1990), vol. I

——, 'Social Contract', in *The Collected Writings of Rousseau*, ed. Roger D. Masters and Christopher Kelly (Hanover, NH, and London, 1994), vol. IV

Saint Jerome, 'Against Jovinianus', in *The Principal Works of St Jerome*, trans. W. H. Fremantle (Oxford, 1893), vol. VI

Schumacher, Ernst Friedrich, *Small Is Beautiful: Economics as if People Mattered* (London, 2010)

Segall, Ken, *Insanely Simple: The Obsession That Drives Apple's Success* (New York, 2012)

'The Shepherd of Hermas', in *The Apostolic Fathers*, trans. Joseph Barber Lightfoot (New York, 1891)

Shi, David E., *The Simple Life: Plain Living and High Thinking in American Culture* (Athens, GA, 2007)

Slobodkin, Lawrence B., *Simplicity and Complexity in the Games of the Intellect* (Cambridge, MA, 1992)

Spenner, Patrick, and Karen Freeman, 'To Keep Your Customers, Keep It Simple', *Harvard Business Review* (May 2012), pp. 109–14

Stein, Stephen J., *The Shaker Experience in America: A History of the United Society of Believers* (New Haven, CT, and London, 1992)

Summary View of the Millennial Church (Albany, NY, 1823)

Testament of Issachar, in *Ante-Nicene Fathers: The Writings of the Fathers down to A.D. 325* (New York, 1903), vol. VIII

The Shepherd of Hermas, in *The Apostolic Fathers*, trans. Joseph Barber Lightfoot (New York, 1981)

Thoreau, Henry David, 'Walden', in *Henry David Thoreau*, ed. Robert F. Sayre (New York, 1985), pp. 321–587

——, 'A Week on the Concord and Merrimack Rivers', ibid., pp. 1–319

Trump, Donald, *The Art of the Deal* (New York, 1987)

Warde, Paul, *The Invention of Sustainability: Nature and Destiny, c. 1500–1870* (Cambridge, 2018)

Woolman, John, *The Journal of John Woolman* (Gloucester, MA, 1971)
Xenophon, *Memorabilia*, trans. E. C. Marchand (London, 1923)

ACKNOWLEDGEMENTS

The ideas collected here were inspired by books, simple lives and by many unreferenced conversations with friends and colleagues. For their intellectual generosity, I would like to thank Christie McDonald, Virginie Greene, Gary Wihl, Philip Lewis, Eric Méchoulan, Barbara Lebrun, Matthew Jefferies, Ursula Tidd and Lisa Guenther. Thank you to Susan P. Johnson, copy-editor extraordinaire, for her meticulous reading of the manuscript. At Reaktion, the encouragement of Ben Hayes at the start of the project and the support of Michael Leaman and Amy Salter in the last phases of the book were much appreciated. Thank you to Julia and Nigel for letting my little companion and me sit under the oak tree and survey the Peaks for hours on end. In moments of hesitation, Kirk Smith was here to offer clarity and support. Thank you. No sincere acknowledgements, no pages, no words without simple emotions: thank you, Patty.